Vocabulous Throwdown™

Now Entering: The Word Zone

Volume 1

By:
Matt Quenville &
Sketchi Bill

With SketchiToons® by Sketch Bill

By permission of NExSW, Inc.

AbVocab Publishing, Inc

Santa Fe, New Mexico

No part of this publication may be reproduced or transmitted in any form or by any means, electronic or mechanical, including photocopy, recording or any information storage or retrieval system, without permission in writing from the publisher.

ISBN-13 978-1-7353279-2-1

SketchiToons®in in frames are used by permission by Northeast by Southwest, Inc.
to create the derivative works in the picture frames contained within.
Original Copyright retained by Northeast by Southwest, Inc.

Other Frames include derivative works by Matt Quenville.

Attributions for SketchiToons® and other frames are given in a later section of the book.

Various Illustrations by Sketchi Bill

Cover Art by Sketchi Bill & Matt Quenville

Absolutely Vocabulous, Vocabulous Throwdown, Abvocab and Abvocab Publishing are trademarks of
AbVocab Publishing, Inc

SketchiToons®, Sketchi, Sketchi Bill are trademarks of Northeast by Southwest, Inc.

All other trademarks are the property of their respective companies.

Printing History:
July 2020
10 9 8 7 6 5 4 3 2 1

Table of Contents

Acknowledgements	4
Forward (Author's Note)	5
Brain-o-meter Levels	7
Quotes	9
PC Warning	10
Mains Words, Definitions & Art	11-84
Word Definitions	85-91
Related Words	92-95
Attributions	96-99
About	100

Author Acknowlegements

Matt Quenville acknowledges with pleasure the decent set of genes he received from his father Tom Quenville and mother Susan Quenville. Dad taught the importance of work ethic and mom encouraged the pursuit of this book and was always a champion of education. Both Tom & Sue raised their kids to think independently and not be boxed in by dogmatism and ideology. Also want to acknowledge the role happenstance plays in life. Tom introduced Matt to Sketchi Bill (Tom's old college roommate). This book is the result of that collaboration. Also, happenstance that this quarantine time would allow him to take time to pursue a creative piece of work that he would otherwise have not had the time to complete. Finally, would like to give a shout out to my kids Jordan and Ansley and wife Afton for support.

Sketchi Bill proudly acknowledges the wonderful lifetime cast of creative and fun-loving characters he has been fortunate enough to work and play with - and more importantly to learn from. In particular, from his earlier professional life Professor Charles Kruger and Mr. Vincent Moeyersoms. And especially, the exceptional human beings that are his kids, Chris and Jana, and his grandkids Rafa and Sandro. Great thanks to Barbara Hunter-Harmon who has critiqued many sketches and has provided an opportunity for spirited discussions about the widest variety of topics, keeping ideas flowing. Memories and thoughts from these folks and so many others are embedded in the sketches. Without them, Sketchi would never been even close to the line of sanity.

Author's Note

Why read this book? So here's the deal. You gotta take these tests in High School & College that supposedly measure your intelligence and what you have learned. After college, society will fork you over a bill that you will spend the rest of your life paying back, usually with interest. Before I became a teacher, I took these silly ass tests too. Whether or not you get into your favorite college or grad school will partly depend on your score on these tests. The least I can do is make it fun for you to learn stuff and do well on the tests. You'll master these words when you are done reading, fo' sho'. Maybe it will help you get a scholarship or accepted to your favorite college. Or just use the book for some shits & giggles & expand your vocabulary.

These entries include curse words and sexual references here and there because they reflect your life experiences & certainly future ones. If nothing else, all that fortnite & foodie shows and music videos & talking trash on Snapchat & Instagram has prepared you for this approach. This book is unlike any other vocabulary study book out there. It is an uncensored, uninhibited study guide written in your language, in your world, using your slang, ya' hurd.

Seriously, it is important that you do well on these tests. I've prepared much of this material myself, with an eye connecting to your world. This book was co-written by Sketchi Bill, an old, but irreverent and whimsical sort.

So, let's vocabulously throwdown. These tests are important. Enjoy the humor and learn the words.

With best luck,

Matt Quenville

Brain-o-Meter Word Levels

Brain-o-Meter Level 1

Softball word: slightly stimulating, brain still on cruise control

BOM 1

Brain-o-Meter Level 2

Moderately hard: get the juices flowing, stimulating but not much brain pain

BOM 2

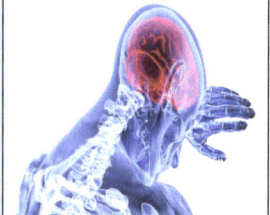

Brain-o-Meter Level 3

Wicked hard: neurons flying, brain is on fire

BOM 3

Brain-o-Meter Level 4

Damn, I can't even pronounce this. My mind is blown. Words of the Elite.

BOM 4

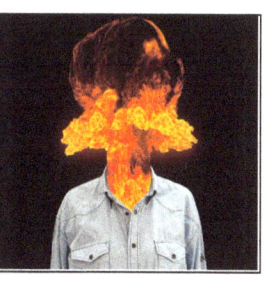

*Brain-o-meter from here on out will be abbreviated as BOM

Quotes

"The more I learn, the more I realize how much I don't know."
Albert Einstein

"Meanwhile the Cosmos is rich beyond measure: the total number of stars in the universe is greater than all the grains of sand on all the beaches of the planet Earth." Carl Sagan

"Do what you can, with what you have, where you are."
Theodore Roosevelt

"I haven't failed. I've just found 10,000 ways that won't work."
Thomas Edison

"Those who are determined to be 'offended' will discover a provocation somewhere. We cannot possibly adjust enough to please the fanatics, and it is degrading to make the attempt."
Christopher Hitchens

"Who controls the past controls the future. Who controls the present controls the past." George Orwell

"Here's all you have to know about men and women; women are crazy, men are stupid. And the main reason women are crazy is that men are stupid" George Carlin

"You can be married and bored, or single and lonely. Ain't no happiness nowhere" Chris Rock

"Common sense is the collection of prejudices acquired by the age of eighteen" Albert Einstein

"It takes considerable knowledge just to realize the extent of your own ignorance" Thomas Sowell

"There are lots of people who mistake their imagination for their memory" Josh Billings

"I want my children to have all of the things I couldn't afford. Then I want to move in with them" Phyllis Diller

Warning: Material may cause you to think and read. Also, if you become offended or laugh out loud or say "I can't believe they actually wrote that" then you are actively engaged and learning, so enjoy becoming Absolutely Vocabulous ™

Astute

The kid was an astute Texas Hold'em poker player, almost as if he had some special super power to sniff out any signs of bluffing or weakness from his opponents.

Astute: ability to read situations & people and turn it to one's advantage

    Synonym: Keen   Antonym: Foolish
    Say What? uh-stoot   BOM 1

Check and Raise all day

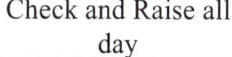

Incorrigible

Catalyte, the alien, was obsessed with keeping his toenails clean. Even though the other aliens never bothered so much as to take a shower, Catalyte always felt the need to stay fresh. He was so adamant about his daily pedicure that he would wait outside the store for hours even while closed. This incorrigible behavior came to an end when his pedicurist refused to give him a pedi because his nails were perfect.

Incorrigible: a person or their tendencies not able to be corrected, improved, or reformed

    Synonym: Intractable   Antonym: Reform
    Say What? in-kawr-i-juh-buh-l   BOM 3

Catalyte about to get his 6 toes a pedi

Effrontery

Mario, Luigi & Yoshi had the effrontery to attack Bowser in Mushroom Kingdom. Mario jumped on his head hoping to hold him back while the others attacked his torso. Little did they know that Bowser, being a father himself, did not want to hurt them so he put them all in very gentle sleep holds.

Effrontery- bold or impertinent behavior

    Synonym: Audacity   Antonym: Caution
    Say What? ih-fruhn-tuh-ree   BOM 3

Absolutely Vocabulous megalomania

Even if you are Steph Curry, paid millions to put the rock in the bucket for three, if you succumb to the **megalomania** induced by mega jersey sales, quickly you will become the team bricklayer, then role player, then bench warmer.

megalomania: false impression of one's own greatness
Synonym: Egotism   Say What? meg-uh-loh-mey-nee-uh   Antonym: Modest

©2020 AbVocab Publishing, Inc. www.facebook.com/abvocab   www.abvocab.com   AbVocab™ with SketchiToons®

Unencumber

Poppa Panda & Bandit the Bird were sick and tired of Smokey the Bear always having the spotlight, so they called up a few of their peeps to have him "taken care of". Unencumbered, these two now rule the forest. "Now who wants to say no to forest fires? That's what we thought."

Unencumber: not having any burden or impediment

    Synonym: Free　　　　Antonym: Burden
    Say What? un-en-kuhm-ber　　　BOM 3

New Sheriffs in Town

Effervescent

Cristiano Ronaldo is the effervescent Portuguese soccer phenom. But did you know that he underwent heart surgery as a teenager? He has helped kids with health problems including paying for the cancer treatment for a 9 year old boy from Spain.

Effervescent: vivacious & enthusiastic
    Synonym: Ebullient   Antonym: Boring
    Say What? eh-fr-veh-snt   BOM 3

Credulous

Henry, drunk and swerving, hoped the officer who was pulling him over would be credulous enough to believe that he was just a bad driver.

Credulous: too willing to believe things
    Synonym: Gullible   Antonym: Suspicious
    Say What? kreh-joo-luhs   BOM 2

Snub

Supergirl, Batman, Wonderwoman & Superman were getting turnt, partying at a remote island when bam, Spiderman descended from above. They had purposely snubbed him but he wasn't going to let this party go on without him.

Snub: give someone the cold shoulder
    Synonym: Scorn   Antonym: Include
    Say What? snuhb   BOM 2

Rapacity

The rapacious, sword wielding, assassin squirrel aggressively hoarded all of the acorns even though he could never eat all of them himself & it meant other squirrels would go hungry.

Rapacity: Excessively Greedy
    Synonym: Voracious Antonym: Abstemious
    Say What? rah-pa-suh-tee   BOM 2

Absolutely Vocabulous: bellicose

With live human sports no longer viable with COVID-19, ESPN has introduced UAF-Ultimate Arthropod Fighting. In episode 1, bellicose ant Conor delivers a fiery speech to his battalion. They enter the ArthrOctagon. Black widow spiders await. Winner take all cage match. Vegas betting line favors the ants.

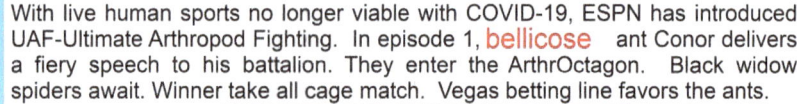

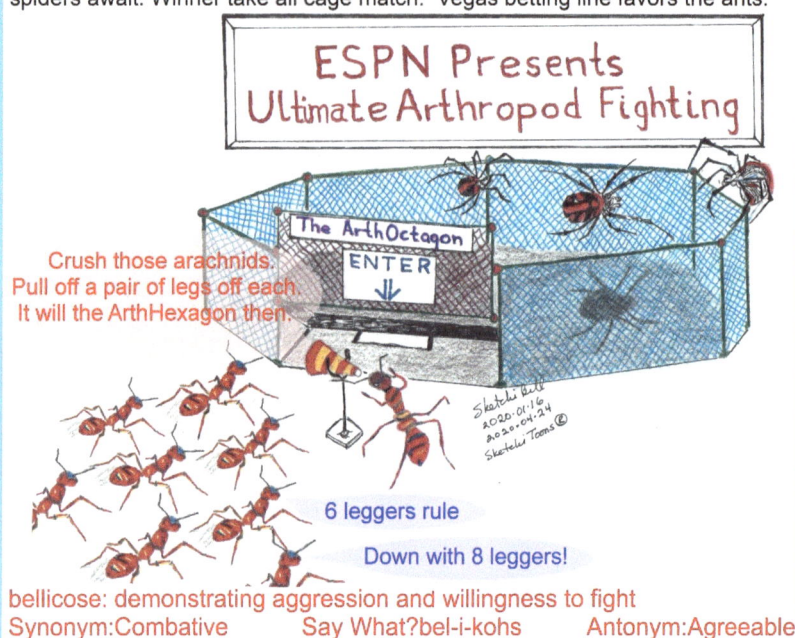

bellicose: demonstrating aggression and willingness to fight
Synonym: Combative   Say What? bel-i-kohs   Antonym: Agreeable

©2020 AbVocab Publishing, Inc. www.facebook.com/abvocab   www.abvocab.com   AbVocab™ with SketchiToons®

Metaphor

On the first date with Samone, Andre felt on the surface cool as a cucumber, but on the inside, a squirrel in traffic.

Metaphor: a thing regarded as representative or symbolic of something else, especially something abstract

Synonym: Analogy   Antonym: Simile
Say What? sim-uh-lee   BOM 2

"I'm so nervous, left, right, straight, what do I do"

Obscure

Steve took his girlfriend Sally to what he thought was an obscure coffee shop. Walking through the front door, he thought he saw an apparition of his chick on the side. But after doing a double take, sure enough, that was her all right. Well I'll be a monkey's bare-assed uncle, talk about getting caught with your pants down he thought.

Obscure: not discovered or known about
    Synonym: Unknown   Antonym: Popular
    Say What? uhb-skyoor   BOM 2

No flippin' way Steve runs in to his sidechick at this obscure coffee shop?

Extrapolate

As Homer finished his 5th Duff Beer by noon Marge extrapolated that at this rate he will be passed out in the lawn by 4PM.

Extrapolate: reasoning the end point based on a trend
    Synonym: Deduce   Antonym: Doubt
    Say What? uhk-stra-puh-leit   BOM 3

Fair extrapolation by Marge

Deliberate

When confronted with the option of going to his in-laws house for the 4th of July or heading on a boys trip to Augusta to work on his Golf game, Todd felt no need to deliberate as he booked aisle A-1 on Delta Air for a non stop flight to Augusta.

Deliberate: long consideration
    Synonym: Ponder   Antonym: Ignore
    Say What? de-lib-er-ate   BOM 1

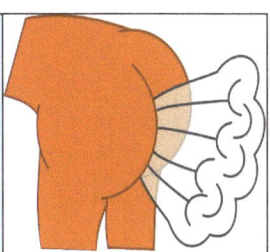

In-Laws or Golf? Not much to deliberate here.

Onomatopoeia

Fart sounds like the sound of air coming out of a butt. Potty humor aside, it is an onomatopoeia.

Onomatopoeia: the formation of a word from a sound associated with what is named
    Say What? on-uh-mat-uh-pee-uh   BOM 3

Absolutely Vocabulous: befuddled BOM 3

Despite months of GPS training and intense psychiatric counseling, the new face of Google Maps was **befuddled** by the simplest request for directions. Forget accurate ETAs or traffic avoidance messages.

befuddle: make (someone) unable to think clearly
Synonym: Bewildered   Say What? bih-fuhdl   Antonym: Lucid

©2020 AbVocab Publishing, Inc. www.facebook.com/abvocab www.abvocab.com AbVocab™ with SketchiToons®

Flabbergasted-Gaffe

The top contenders for the 2020 U.S. Presidential election have left many **flabbergasted**. With a population of over 300 million people, are you telling me that a totalitarian dunce & a walking, or should I say touching, **gaffe** are the best we have to offer?

Flabbergasted: surprised someone greatly
   Synonym: Astonished   Antonym: Calm
   Say What? fla-br-ga-stuhd   BOM 3

Gaffe: an unintentional remark causing shame
   Synonym: Blunder   Antonym: Couth
   Say What? gaf   BOM 2

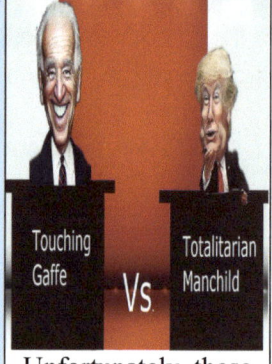

Unfortunately, these are the 2 choices for the 2020 Presidential election

Pun

Example: My brother farted in an elevator, it was wrong on so many levels.
Pun: a joke exploiting the different possible meanings of a word
    Synonym: Double Entendre
    Say What? puhn   BOM 1

Apprehensive

The Chihuahua Ren was sick and tired of always being called apprehensive by Stimpy because of his shaking. "I'm just cold dammit, I'm not scared!"
Apprehensive: anxious, fearful
    Synonym: Afraid   Antonym: Bold
    Say What? a-pree-hen-suhv   BOM 2

Détente

All thoughts of a détente between Ryu & Blair Dame were gone when they resumed their mutual hostility towards each other in the enchanted Forest. Blair knocked him out for good with a swift roundhouse kick.
Détente- the easing of hostility or strained relations, especially between countries
    Synonym: Easement   Antonym: Hostile
    Say What? dey-tahnt   BOM 3

Machination

The humans on planet Earth had no way to know that they would fall victims to the machination devised by 2 aliens plotting their demise.
Machination: a plot or scheme
    Synonym: Conspiracy   Antonym: Innocent
    Say What? ma-kuh-nei-shn   BOM 3

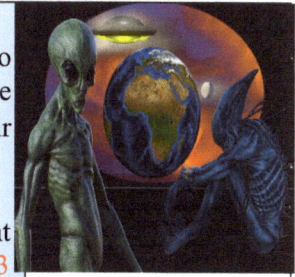

"We will start with Los Angeles"

Absolutely Vocabulous ecclesiastical BOM 3

Jack dreamed of winning NFL bets. His wife rapt with the **ecclesiastical** organ music and stained glass. The boys happily playing FIFA Soccer on their Nintendo Switch. Okay until, on winning, out came a resounding Goooooool.

ecclesiastical: relating to the Christian Church or its clergy
synonym: Churchly   Say What? ih-klee-zee-asti-kuhl   antonym: Secular
©2020 AbVocab Publishing, Inc. www.facebook.com/abvocab   www.abvocab.com   AbVocab™ with SketchiToons®

Lugubrious

The bugs held a lugubrious memorial to all of their fallen comrades who died valiantly as the result of the giant human who pushed some metal contraption with rotating blades across the grass. Ralph was done being sad. He wanted revenge. "Lets destroy that metal thing with blades!"

Lugubrious: looking or sounding sad
   Synonym: Mournful   Antonym: Joyful
   Say What? luh-goo-bree-uhs   BOM 3

Eradicate

Alita Battle Angel is a cyborg who wakes up in a new body with no memory of her past. In the final battle she eradicates Grewishka by slicing him in half. "I do not stand by in the presence of evil".

Eradicate: destroy completely
   Synonym: Annihilate   Antonym: Capitulate
   Say What? ih-rad-i-keyt   BOM 2

Adroit-Deft

Is there a better fighting match-up than this? The adroit and notorious UFC fighter Connor Mcgregor lost to the deft & efficient flyweight pretty boy boxer Floyd Mayweather in 2017. There are rumors they will fight again. Who will win this time around?

Adroit: skillfull using the hands or mind
   Synonym: Adept   Antonym: Clumsy
   Say What? uh-droit   BOM 2

Deft: skillful and quick in one's movement
   Synonym   Antonym: Inept
   Say What? deft   BOM 2

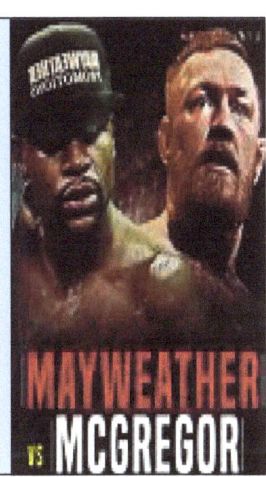

Malediction

Evanora the evil witch laid a malediction on the entire town when she uttered "funnel, wind, destroy" unleashing cyclones galore. This small town was doomed.

Malediction: a magical word or phrase uttered with the intention of bringing about evil or destruction; a curse
   Synonym: Hex   Antonym: Blessing
   Say What? mal-i-dik-shuhn   BOM 3

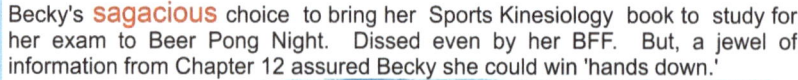

Absolutely Vocabulous — sagacious  BOM 3

Becky's **sagacious** choice to bring her Sports Kinesiology book to study for her exam to Beer Pong Night. Dissed even by her BFF. But, a jewel of information from Chapter 12 assured Becky she could win 'hands down.'

sagacious: having or showing keen good judgment
Synonym: Judicious   Say What? suh-gey-shuhs   Antonym: Careless
©2020 AbVocab Publishing, Inc. www.facebook.com/abvocab   www.abvocab.com   AbVocab™ with SketchiToons®

Multifaceted

Clawdeen Wolf is a *multifaceted* warewolf from Monster's High that can play soccer, track & field & baseball at a high level. She is also a talented fashion desingner with her own fashion show! Her bff's Frankie Stein & Draculaura always got her back. She can be fierce but normally she is kind.

Multifaceted: having many talents
   Synonym: Versatile   Antonym: Limited
   Say What? muhl-tee-fas-i-tid   BOM 3

Incredulous

The dinosaurs must have had an incredulous look on their faces as the asteroid was beaming towards earth. They had roamed the planet for 165 million years and all of a sudden, bam!
Incredulous: a person or their manner unwilling or unable to believe something
    Synonym: Disbelief   Antonym: Believe
    Say What: in-krej-uh-luhs   BOM 2

"Oh Flip. This can't be happening!"

Quixotic

After spending her childhood watching chick flicks, soap operas & magical fairytales featuring knights, princes & castles, the guys at the bar just didn't quite stack up to her quixotic fantasies.
Quixotic: foolishly romantic
    Synonym: Dreamy   Antonym: Practical
    Say What? kwuhk-saa-tuhk   BOM 3

"I'll be your knight and shining armor"

Captivate

Dylan, the 14 year old boy, was completely captivated after the movie caption warning stated "contains violence, nudity & language not suitable for children, viewer discretion advised".
Captivate: attract & hold the attention of
    Synonym: Enthrall   Antonym: Bored
    Say What? kap-tuh-veit   BOM 2

"Yes! Nudity!"

Pernicious

Larry the mad scientist was hoping to create a cure for cancer but instead created a pernicious compound making his hair green and fall out.
Pernicious: having a harmful effect, usually gradual or subtle.
    Synonym: Noxious   Antonym: Beneficial
    Say What? pr-ni-shuhs   BOM 3

 **shrewd**

Self-proclaimed 'Greatest Of All Time,' Lucas thought he was so **shrewd** to date three girls at the same time. But, on the first day of March Madness he realized that he might have been too casual passing out apartment keys.

shrewd: showing sharp intellect and judgment
Synonym: Astute   Say What? shrood   Antonym: Obtuse

©2020 AbVocab Publishing, Inc. www.facebook.com/abvocab   www.abvocab.com   AbVocab™ with SketchiToons®

Exuberant

There was a trio of exuberance at the final Little League baseball game. The player who had been hitless all year finally got on base with a single, the Dad's celebrated in the bleachers with a cooler full of cold beer & the umpire would be calling his final game of the year. Rejoice!

Exuberant: joyous
    Synonym: Ebullient   Antonym: Miserable
    Say What? ig-zoo-br-uhnt   BOM 2

"I'll be so exuberant when this damn game is over."

Epitome

Flash, Goku, Roadrunner & Sonic lined up for the race of a lifetime. Who would win and be known forever as the epitome of speed? Not going out on a limb by saying Flash would win.
Epitome: a person or thing the is the perfect example of a particular quality
    Synonym: Embodiment Antonym: Opposite
    Say What? ih-pit-uh-mee   BOM 2

Speed is my game   Let's fight it out   Meep Meep   Up, over and gone

Euphoric

Sally the worker bee was dreading work this Saturday. Just when she was thinking about how she would have to feed the drones & collect the pollen she felt euphoric when she heard that Saturday would be a honeycomb party and she would have the day off!
Euphoric: intense feeling of excitement
    Synonym: Elated   Antonym: Sad
    Say What? yoo-fo-rik   BOM 2

"Did somebody say honey party! Hell Yea."

Jovial-Misanthrope-Paroxysm

Santa Claus was usually a jovial man. However, around Christmas time, the pressures of the job really got to him. His whiskey intake went up drastically, he had sudden paroxysms of anger usually directed at the elves for not working hard enough and was a real bastard to Mrs. Claus. He couldn't help being a misanthrope for 1 month out of the year.
Jovial: cheerful and friendly
    Synonym: Chipper   Antonym: Angry
    Say What? joh-vee-uhl   BOM 2
Misanthrope: hater of mankind
    Synonym: Hater   Antonym: Lover
    Say What? mi-suhn-throwp   BOM 3
Paroxysm: a sudden violent outburst
    Synonym: Spasm   Antonym: Calm
    Say What? par-uh-k-siz-uh m   BOM 3

Santa after a long night of boozing

"I soon as I nurse this hangover, those elves are gonna get a tongue lashing!"

Absolutely Vocabulous — frenetic

BOM 2

The **frenetic** middle school classroom housed a toxic brew of undeveloped prefrontal cortices, an inhumane student to teacher ratio and a interim principal who thought corporal punishment was still a possibility.

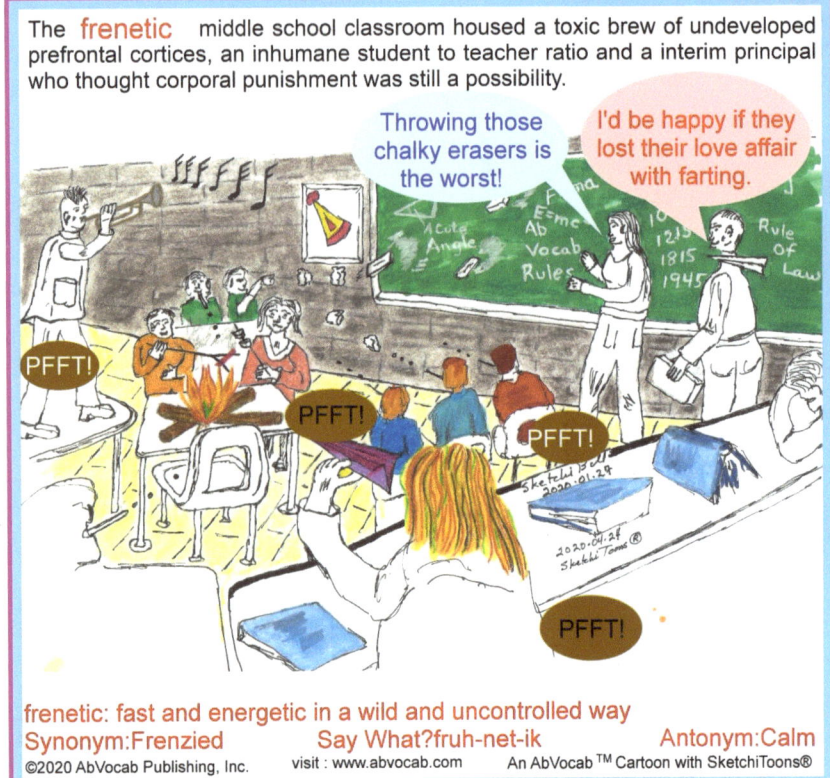

frenetic: fast and energetic in a wild and uncontrolled way
Synonym: Frenzied   Say What? fruh-net-ik   Antonym: Calm
©2020 AbVocab Publishing, Inc.   visit : www.abvocab.com   An AbVocab ™ Cartoon with SketchiToons®

Trepidation

Micah the Meercat felt a surge of trepidation when he heard a noise. "Oh please don't tell me there is snake, I just want to chill by the cactus today. Yep, it's a snake. Perfectly still!"

Trepidation: fear of something
  Synonym: Dismay   Antonym: Relaxed
  Say What? treh-pi-dei-shn   BOM 2

"If I don't move it won't see me."

Prototype

Jeremy Lin, an Asian point guard & Harvard grad, is not your prototypical NBA basketball player.

Prototype: a first, typical or preliminary model of something, from which other forms are developed or copied

    Synonym: Template   Antonym: Copy
    Say What? proh-tuh-tahyp   BOM 2

Jeremy is probably too smart for the NBA

Officious

Ralph the PE teacher, aggressively lashed out at the student for not throwing the dodgeball hard enough. This officious attitude made him come across as some kind of bizarre, abnormally excited, apelike figure.

Officious: domineering over trivial matters

    Synonym: Dictatorial   Antonym: Casual
    Say What? uh-fi-shuhs   BOM 3

"If you hit a kid in the face with the dodgeball, u get extra credit"

Antipathy

Dan was an easygoing dude but has an intense antipathy towards the sound an alarm clock makes, which is coincidentally the same sound his wife Selma makes when she is nagging him he thought.

Antipathy: strong dislike

    Synonym: Odium   Antonym: Affinity
    Say What? an-ti-puh-thee   BOM 2

"Why does she keep talking? I hate that sound."

Disdain

Dan's wife Selma is a sweet gal but has disdain for the sound a freight train makes which is coincidentally the sound Dan makes when he snores she thought.

Disdain: something or someone not worthy of respect

    Synonym: Derision   Antonym: Admiration
    Say What? duhs-dein   BOM 3

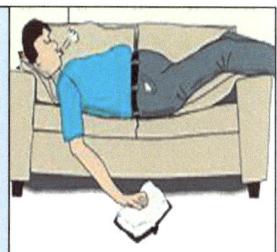

Selma kicked him to the couch.

Absolutely Vocabulous gouge BOM 2

Stopping at the convenience store for a quick lunch, the signs showed that this store was preying on panic. Price **gouging** for sure. Jane will remember they did this and never go back. $60 for Charmin - leaves would do the job.

gouge: overcharge; swindle; make a groove, hole, or indentation
Synonym: Swindle   Say What? gouj   Antonym: Help

©2020 AbVocab Publishing, Inc. www.facebook.com/abvocab   www.abvocab.com AbVocab™ with SketchiToons®

Abdicate

The toddler monkeys Max & Manga didn't feel like they had to listen to their dad Tony so they abdicated their chores to throw out their banana peels. Tony was not happy & threatened them with a rock.

Abdicate: to fail to fulfill responsibilities
   Synonym: Relinquish   Antonym: Fulfill
   Say What? ab-duh-keit   BOM 3

Clean up your dang blasted banana peels boys!

Utopia

The bulldog Sir Chewsalot was sound asleep in his bed in **REM 3**. He was dreaming of squirrels, hickory smoked beef bones, chasing cats & chewing up that delicious shoe. Ahhhh, what a utopia he thought. Wait, am I dreaming of chewing that shoe or did I actually…smack! His owner hit him with a rolled up newspaper across the butt because he had some fun munching on that shoe before he dozed off.

Utopia: ideal place and life
    Synonym: Paradise   Antonym: Dystopia
    Say What? yoo-toh-pee-uh   BOM 2

Rapid Eye Movement (REM 3)- deep sleep, with rapid movement of the eyes & dreams

"I love the taste of leather!" What a Utopia.

Acerbic

Give me your phone now the mother said in an acerbic tone, snatching the iphone away from the teen. The invincibility faded from the teen's face as she realized she couldn't facetime her bff or check the location of her boyfriend Bobby on Snapchat.

Acerbic: forthright way of speaking
    Synonym: Scathing   Antonym: Mild
    Say What? uh-ser-buhk   BOM 2

"OMG that beyotch is being way extra. I can't even find out where Bobby is!"

Indignant

The Granny Smith green apple was indignant after discovering through a poll test that it was the least favorite apple compared to Red Delicious, Fuji, & Golden Delicious. Head spokesperson for the green apple stated in a press release, "Man, this is racist".

Indignant: angered at unfair treatment
    Synonym: Aggrieved   Antonym: Content
    Say What? uhn-dig-nuhnt   BOM 2

"It's cause I'm green isn't it?"

Absolutely Vocabulous — inane

BOM 2

As a teacher, there are some things to keep quiet. Bad enough that they knew I was Alvin Monk. But, when they learned my middle name was Chip, even Jeff my best student began doing the most **inane** things. Worse than substituting.

Speech bubbles:
- AP History Mr. A. Monk
- Jeff, you're way behind. Get stuffin' those nuts in your cheek.
- Love those Chip Monk Tails!
- Sarah, 2 more and you've got the class record.

inane: silly and pointless; stupid; empty; insubstantial
Synonym: fatuous   Say What? ih-neyn   Antonym: Intelligent

©2020 AbVocab Publishing, Inc. www.facebook.com/abvocab www.abvocab.com AbVocab™ with SketchiToons®

Distraught

The Seattle Seahawks fan was so **distraught** after they lost their playoff game that he didn't get out of bed for a week. Football induced depression is only a real thing in Seattle.

Distraught: deeply upset & agitated
  Synonym: Agitated   Antonym: Tranquil
  Say What? duh-straat   BOM 2

"I can't believe they lost! My life is over."

Impeccable

The high school sophomore spent an hour impeccably writing an early dismissal note that looked identical to her mother's handwriting.
Impeccable: faultless
  Synonym: Flawless   Antonym: Defective
  Say What? im-pek-uh-buhl   BOM 2

"Off to the beach beatches, sun's out buns out"

Coy

Izuku Midoriya is the main character in My Hero Academia. He is a coy & insecure boy who is bullied at school because he doesn't possess any 'quirks'. After developing a 'quirk', he is able to stockpile potential energy of raw power that can be unleashed into kinetic energy of strength, speed, agility, & durability allowing him to levitate.
Coy: Shyness or Modesty
  Synonym: Bashful   Antonym: Aggressive
  Say What? koi   BOM 2
Potential Energy: Stored Energy
Kinetic Energy: Energy of Motion

"It's alright, I will save you, never give up!"

Enchanted

Unlike his single buddies, Liam only went after cougars. He was enchanted by their stretch marks, low cut tops from the 90's, heavy blue eye shadow, extra dangly wizard sleeves, voluptuous child bearing hips, saucer sized areolas & the real difference maker, a real job.
Enchanted: placed under a spell; charmed
  Synonym: Bewitched   Antonym: Repel
  Say What? uhn-chan-tuhd   BOM 2
Areola: ring of pigmented skin around the nipple
Wizard Sleeve:
large, hanging or dangling labia

Cougar- an older attractive woman

29

Absolutely Vocabulous — **deleterious**

The morning after, Al sat on the toilet experiencing the **deleterious** effects of three buckets of Buffalo Wings and of too many 'car bombs' at his promotion party at the local sports bar. Thankfully, it was Saturday morning.

Perhaps a morning after Bloody Mary would help.

deleterious : harmful, often in a subtle or unexpected way
Synonym: Noxious   Say What? del-i-teer-ee-uhs   Antonym: Beneficial

©2020 AbVocab Publishing, Inc. www.facebook.com/abvocab   www.abvocab.com   AbVocab™ with SketchiToons®

Nebulous

Sarah had a **nebulous** idea of what she was looking for in a guy. Actually no, let me take that back. It is very specific: 6 foot 4 inches tall, black hair, 8 pack abs, a sense of humor with a 6 figure salary but also enough time off from work to be with her and the kids.

Nebulous: hazy, cloudy
  Synonym: Vague   Antonym: Specific
  Say What? neh-byoo-luhs   BOM 3

Eh, he'll do

Arbiter

The two old timers stood on their property lines in a dispute over territory. They waved their canes at each other and called each other names "shmuck" said one, "moron" said the other. Finally the wives came out and played arbiters "get your old asses inside, lunch is ready".

Arbiter: a person who settles a dispute
    Synonym: Judge
    Say What? ahr-bi-ter   BOM 2

"Mornin' Schmuck Mornin' Moron"

Flamboyant

Fantasia the fabulous, flamboyant drag queen flaunted his pink flamingo frock down New York City's fashion week runway.

Flamboyant: a person tending to attract attention because of their exuberance, confidence, and stylishness
    Synonym: Extravagant   Antonym: Plain
    Say What? flam-boy-uhnt   BOM 2

Fabulously flamboyant wouldn't u say?

Aloof

Dorthy the Democrat & Ronald the Republican watched Jeopardy every Thursday night. Ronald would shout out the answers proving his hearing was fine but when Dorthy asked him about his stance on the upcoming Presidential election he became suspiciously aloof. "What? I just can't hear you", he would say.

Aloof: distant, remote
    Synonym: Detached   Antonym: Friendly
    Say What? uh-loof   BOM 2

"What Dorthy? I can't hear you, is dinner ready?"

Absolutely Vocabulous — eviscerate  BOM 2

Joan realized it was because of his job at the meat processing plant that her hubby was desensitized and watch, with no emotion, the scene in Braveheart where Mel Gibson was **eviscerated**. Alba gu bràth (Scotland Forever!)

eviscerate: disembowel (person or animal); deprive (something) of its essence
Synonym: Disembowel   Say What? ih-vis-uh-reyt   Antonym: Protect

©2020 AbVocab Publishing, Inc. www.facebook.com/abvocab   www.abvocab.com   AbVocab™ with SketchiToons®

Sycophant

Tiffany had all of her sycophant bff's praising her in the hallway. Vote for Tiffany for class president, she is so cute! OMG, she broke her hair tie, how will she ever survive in gym class today. This is an emergency, we have got to find her one.

Sycophant: to suck up to gain favor
   Synonym: Lackey   Antonym: Independent
   Say What? si-kuh-fnt   BOM 3

"OMG, like, Vote for Tiffany kk!"

Exalt

The Kangaroo exalted the world record holder for highest jump on a pogo stick which stands at 11.15 feet. "Man, if someone gave me one of those jumpy poles, just imagine, my ass would be over the trees!"

Exalt: hold something in high regard
    Synonym: Laud   Antonym: Disparage
    Say What? uhg-zaalt   BOM 2

"Give me a jumpy stick & see how high I can jump"

Inconceivable

It is inconceivable that the world's shortest bodybuilder, Aditya Dev, a 2 foot 9 inch Indian dwarf, could lift 5X his body weight!

Inconceivable: can't be imagined
    Synonym: Improbable Antonym: Believable
    Say What? in-kuhn-see-vuh-bl   BOM 2

Primordial Dwarfism- is a rare and dangerous group of genetic conditions that result in a small body size.

Frenzy-Involuntary-Extol

Young girls all over the world got lost in a frenzy when K Pop boy band BTS arrived unannounced. Some cried, some spoke in tongues, some screamed and others had involuntary muscle spasms almost as if they were having a seizure. "OMG Jin & V are so cuuttttee the girls extolled".

Frenzy: uncontrolled state or situation
    Synonym: Turmoil Antonym: Equanamity
    Say What? fren-zee   BOM 3

Involuntary: done without conscious control
    Synonym: Reflex Antonym: Intentional
    Say What? ihn-vaa-luhn-the-ree   BOM 2

Extol: praise enthusiastically
    Synonym: Applaud Antonym: Criticize
    Say What? ek-stowl   BOM 2

Girls go into a frenzy, completely losing their minds when they see boy band BTS

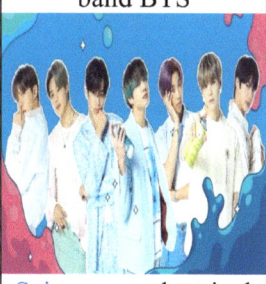

Seizure: an electrical disturbance in the brain causing involuntary muscle spasms.

Absolutely Vocabulous — expedite   BOM 2

V.P. Pence delivered on his directive to **expedite** the delivery of sophisticated test equipment by Mr. Trump in time for the National Park Service to adhere to the 'social distancing' directives, in time for the 'bump' trails received in usage.

Smokey Says: Don't burn the poles!

expedite: make something happen sooner or quicker
Synonym: Hasten   Say What? ek-spi-dahyt   Antonym: Hinder

©2020 AbVocab Publishing, Inc. www.facebook.com/abvocab www.abvocab.com AbVocab™ with SketchiToons®

Alliteration

The carnivorous corona virus carrying cow contaminated the cattle.

Alliteration - using the same letter or sound at the beginning of each word in a sentence
  Synonym: Repetition
  Say What? uh-lit-uh-rey-shuhn   BOM 2

"I ain't got no Corona Virus!"

Audacious

Zena was a warrior princess. She was audacious when fighting gnomes, skeletons and monsters and was known throughout villages and towns as one who don't play that shit. But she took off this particular day to get a mani-pedi. "I gotta look pretty when kicking ass."

Audacious- to take bold risks
  Synonym: Courageous Antonym: Cowardly
  Say What? aa-dei-shuhs   BOM 2

"I would look so cute if I did my nails before battle."

Unassuming-Echelon

Peyton Manning is a nice guy off the gridiron with unassuming humor & an aww-shucks demeanor but nasty on the field, passing with surgical precision & picking apart defenses. He is one of a few QB's on the same echelon as Tom Brady.

Unassuming: not claiming attention
  Synonym: Self-Deprecate Antonym: Cocky
  Say What? Uhn-uh-soo-ming   BOM 2
Echelon: a level in an organization
  Synonym: Level Antonym: Disorganization
  Say What? eh-shuh-laan   BOM 2

"I'm going to thread this needle with a smile on my face."

Burly

Russia's top strongman Elbrus Nigmatullin is known as the Russian Hercules for a reason. In 2016, he stopped a galloping horse with his bare hands. Yes, you read that correctly. He also pulls tanks & mac trucks with ease. Elbrus could be described as burly, with a big boned frame and massive muscles but there really is no word to describe this guy.

Burly: a person large and strong built
  Synonym: Stocky   Antonym: Scrawny
  Say What? bur-lee   BOM 1

Burly for sure, maybe even Herculean.

Absolutely Vocabulous — hedonist BOM 3

Hedonists Jack and Diane misread the blurb about the Tibet retreat with the ascetic Monks. Arriving at the Tashihunpo Monastery they found out they had to eschew cigs, drugs, liquor, sex and leave all luggage behind. Sucks big time.

> Om Om Om Om
>
> Desire is the root of all suffering. Embrace chanting.
>
> No Booze! No Smokes! WTF!
>
> No Luggage. But a sacred robe.
>
> Shit, I brought my sexiest Dresses.

hedonist: a person who acts purely in the pursuit of pleasure
Synonym: Debauchee   Say What? heed-n-ist   Antonym: Ascetic

©2020 AbVocab Publishing, Inc. www.facebook.com/abvocab   www.abvocab.com   AbVocab™ with SketchiToons®

Aphorism

"He's not really stupid, he just has bad luck when he thinks."

Aphorism - a pithy observation that contains a general truth
  Synonym: Saying
  Say What? a-fr-i-zm   BOM 3

"I already forgot what I was thinking"

Dexterity-Musculo-Skeletal

Giannis Antetokounmpo, aka the Greek Freak, dazzles the crowd with elegance and power as he glides through the lane and dunks over another helpless opponent. With a wingspan that resembles Elastigirl from the Incredibles & huge hands exhibiting dexterity as he swallows the basketball like a peach, Giannis has a musculo-skeletal system perfectly fine-tuned for hoopin'.

Dexterity: skill using hands while doing tasks
    Synonym: Finesse   Antonym: Clumy
    Say What? dek-ster-i-tee   BOM 2

Musculo-Skeletal: Muscles & Skeleton
    Synonym: Musculature
    Say What? muh-skyuh-low-skeh-luh-tl
    BOM 3

Good luck stopping that freak.

Fraught

Androm the alien was sent to NYC to take notes on human behavior & report back. He concluded: "Very peculiar. Fraught with anxiety, they work all day & chase green paper. They fight wars & argue over nothing at all, peculiar indeed."

Fraught: causing or affected by anxiety or stress
    Synonym: Overwrought   Antonym: Empty
    Say What? Frawt   BOM 2

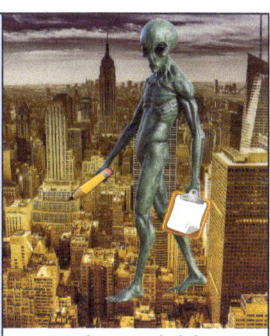

Androm visiting NYC

Cattywampus

Crecilda the crazy cat lady kept her house all cattywampus with cats, clutter and miscellaneous jank everywhere.

Cattywampus: skewed, sideways or out of alignment
    Synonym: Cockeyed   Antonym: Orderly
    Say What? kat-ee-wom-puh-s   BOM 4

Absolutely Vocabulous **illusion** BOM 2

Out of shape Rodney was under the *illusion* that he was 'Mr. Suave' on the dance foor. 'Bro' Gordon had the delusion that he would bed the sexy redhead.

"Gordo. Bro. Do I know how To Boogie!"

"Rod, Dude. that redhead wants my bod!"

illusion: something wrongly perceived or interpreted by the senses
Synonym: Fantasy   Say What? ih-loo-zhuhn   Antonym: Reality
©2020 AbVocab Publishing, Inc. www.facebook.com/abvocab   www.abvocab.com   AbVocab™ with SketchiToons®

Disheveled

When Olivia woke up, she took a shower and looked in the mirror and thought something looked different but couldn't figure out what. Oh of course, I forgot to take the towel off my head. No longer looking *disheveled* in her opinion, it was now time to take the kids to school.

Disheveled: untidy hair, clothes, or appearance
  Synonym: Ragged   Antonym: Clean
  Say What? dih-shev-uhld   BOM 3

Olivia, a bit disheveled this morning.

Versatile

Taylor Swift may be known for her pop/country voice but she can also play guitar, banjo, piano, ukulele, electric guitar, writes poetry & loves history. Talk about being versatile & quite the catch!

Versatile: able to adapt to many different functions or activities
    Synonym: Talented   Antonym: Limited
    Say What? vur-suh-tl   BOM 2

Ms.Versatile can do it all

Panache

The Brazilian soccer team has the ability to not just beat you, but beat you with a show of panache. They possess strong team unity, skillful ball control and a rare capacity to play hard but almost look like they aren't trying. Speaking of panache, check out those Brazilian girls wearing bikinis!

Panache: flamboyant confidence of style
    Synonym: Brio   Antonym: Boring
    Say What? puh-nash   BOM 3

Pele...& whoa

Demigod-Protean

IT, aka Pennywise the dancing killer clown, is a demigod who preys on little children. This protean monster is able to shape-shift into your worst nightmare.

Demigod: offspring of a god and a mortal
    Synonym: Powerful   Antonym: Mortal
    Say What? dem-ee-god   BOM 2

Protean- tending to change frequently
    Synonym: Shape-Shifter Antonym: Constant
    Say What? proh-tee-uh n   BOM 3

"Would you like a balloon g-g-g georgie. We all float down here, you'll float too"

Absolutely Vocabulous — impunity

It seems crazy, but telling the truth seems to have become obsolete, with some people thinking they can pass off all sorts of drivel with *impunity*. But some folks honor their fiduciary responsibilities to their job goals.

Speech: "If you insist that Tom and Kate count in the census, I will have to have an inspector come."

Speech: "WELL, Cats ARE PEOPLE TOO!"

Speech: "I'm sorry, but you are not Trump doing a news conference!"

impunity: exempt from punishment; freedom from consequences
Synonym: Freedom   Say What? im-pyoo-ni-tee   Antonym: Prohibition

©2020 AbVocab Publishing, Inc. www.facebook.com/abvocab   www.abvocab.com   AbVocab™ with SketchiToons®

Esoteric

The *esoteric* Illuminati has captured the minds of young people today. So who is this mystical organization? Well, nobody knows jack. They are supposedly lurking behind every corner, secretly listening in on conversations, controlling the world economy & still have time to rig all the bingo games at nursing homes throughout America.

Esoteric - intended for or likely to be understood by only a small number of people
Synonym: Recondite   Antonym: Clear
Say What? es-uh-ter-ik   BOM 3

The Illuminati is controlling everything eh? How about some evidence?

Stolid-Equanimity

The bomb defusing company was interviewing for candidates. They top criteria was that they had to be completely stolid under pressure. To weed out the weaklings, candidates were first taken to a daycare and exposed to screaming babies and toddlers. The candidates who showed perfect equanimity were instantly hired.

Stolid: a person who is calm, dependable, and showing little emotion or animation
    Synonym: Tough   Antonym: Anxious
    Say What? stol-id   BOM 2

Equanimity: mental calmness in a bad situation
    Synonym: Unflappable   Antonym: Anxiety
    Say What? ee-kwuh-ni-muh-tee   BOM 3

"After getting through Daycare, defusing this is a piece of cake"

Formidable-Nemesis

Iron man, with his special powers of strength, flying, rays shot out of his palms & armor suit make him a formidable nemesis to Minotaur.

Formidable: inspiring fear or respect through being large, powerful, intense, or capable
    Synonym: Capable   Antonym: Weak
    Say What? for-muh-duh-bl   BOM 3

Nemesis: the inescapable agent of someone's or something's downfall
    Synonym: Arch Enemy   Antonym: Ally
    Say What? neh-muh-suhs   BOM 2

"I Love You 3000"

Petulant

As Queen Quatilda stood next to her GWagin in the driveway of her million dollar mansion, she petulantly wined to her 80 year old husband that their mansion & car weren't big enough.

Petulant: a person chilishly sulky or whiny
    Synonym: Cranky   Antonym: Agreeable
    Say What? peh-chuh-luhnt   BOM 2

"It's just not big enough darling"

41

Absolutely Vocabulous — infusion BOM 2

Transferring his last personal $2M to keep his company solvent through the coronavirus crisis, captain of industry Golde McNugget began to think of **infusions** other than of cash. Yum, Peach Vodka martini. Boo, Needles.

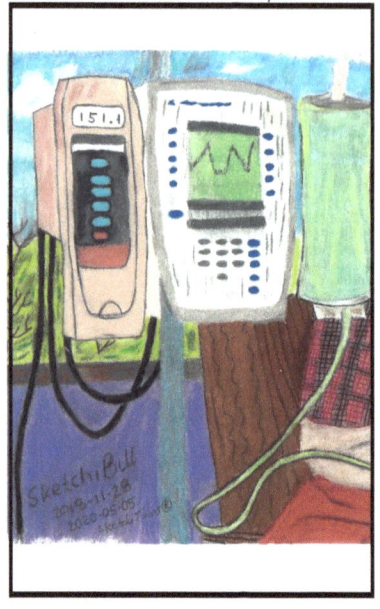

infusion: drink made by soaking something in a liquid; introduce something new
Synonym: Concoction   Say What? in-fyoo-zhuhn   Antonym: Drain

©2020 AbVocab Publishing, Inc. www.facebook.com/abvocab   www.abvocab.com AbVocab™ with SketchiToons®

Surreptitious-Pilfer

The bird swooped down and **surreptitiously** stole the **carrion** right out of the other bird's mouth. "You narrow beaked **pilfering** bastard!"

Surreptitious: secretive
  Synonym: Clandestine   Antonym: Open
  Say What? sur-uh p-tish-uh-s   BOM 3

Pilfer: to steal, especially in small quantities
  Synonym: Purloin   Antonym: Give
  Say What? pil-fer   BOM 2

Carrion: the decaying flesh of dead animals

You pilfering bastard, that's my my carrion!

42

Valiant-Spectacle-Morph

It is quite the spectacle to see how the definition of bravery has morphed over the years. Bravery used to mean toughness in the face of danger. You know, go to war, live thru a Great Depression, get teeth pulled without Novocain, shit like that. Today, we think we are acting valiantly in quarantine in our homes with alcohol, snacks & Netflix.

Valiant: showing courage
    Synonym: Fearless   Antonym: Scared
    Say What? va-lee-uhnt   BOM 2

Spectacle: impressive visual impact
    Synonym: Display   Antonym: Normality
    Say What? spek-tuh-kuhl   BOM 2

Morph: to change from one form to another
    Synonym: Contort   Antonym: Stagnate
    Say What? Mawrf   BOM 2

"Look at me, I'm a national hero. I'm so valiant! I think I need some more popcorn. Now where is my stimulus check?"

Grave-Mortify

Emily the teen was in a grave situation. The pimple on her forehead had grown and it was picture day at school. She was mortified. OMG! Everyone is going to be looking at me she thought, but in fact, at this exact time, 100 other girls at her school were thinking the same thing.

Grave: serious or dangerous
    Synonym: Serious   Antonym: Trivial
    Say What? grave   BOM 1

Mortify: great embarrassment & shame
    Synonym- Humiliate   Antonym: Happy
    Say What? mawr-tuh-fahy   BOM 2

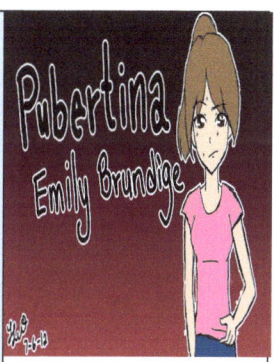

"Nooooo, this can't be happening. The pimple grew! Big Yikes."

Absolutely Vocabulous: scatalogical

Although he had absconded to Tampa Bay, Tom Brady took his chiseled features to a Boston pub expecting a warm welcome. New England women take their sports seriously, but being Absolutely Vocabulous, they articulated their thoughts about this Benedict Arnold without scatalogical references.

scatalogical: obscenity, especially words or humor referring to excrement
Synonym: Bawdy   Say What? skuh-tol-uh-jee   Antonym: Decent

©2020 AbVocab Publishing, Inc. www.facebook.com/abvocab   www.abvocab.com   AbVocab™ with SketchiToons®

Inoculate

So, you take a dead or weakened virus and inject it into your body. Sounds crazy right? That's exactly what a vaccine is. Once inoculated, your body memorizes that germ so it can fight it next time.

Inoculate: vaccinate to become immune
   Synonym: Immunize   Antonym: Contract
   Say What? ih-nok-yuh-leyt   BOM 2

Looks painful but better than getting the disease right?

Prepossessing-Envious-Swoon

Chris Hemsworth, whooowhea is he a beefcake. He has all of the prepossessing features that make men envious and women swoon; the hairline, the strong jawline, the rugged features and the deep throated Austrilian accent make him irresistible.

Prepossessing: attractive in appearance
    Synonym: Winsome   Antonym: Ugly
    Say What? pree-puh-zeh-suhng   BOM 3

Envious: a feeling resent aroused by someone else's possessions, qualities, or luck
    Synonym: Resentful   Antonym: Content
    Say What? en-vee-uhs   BOM 2

Swoon: faint from extreme emotion
    Synonym: Lightheaded   Antonym: Lucid
    Say What? swoon   BOM

"I have all the prepossessing characteristics. Do you think just anyone could play Thor?"

Insipid

You know how I know for a fact that Brussel Sprouts suck? When the CoronaVirus made people act crazy and buy up everything in grocery stores the only thing left was Brussel Sprouts. They are insipid little green balls of nastiness unless drenched in garlic and oil and grilled and even then, they still suck.

Insipid: lacking flavor or vigor
    Synonym: Bland   Antonym: Tasty
    Say What? uhn-si-puhd   BOM 2

Yep, only thing left in the store was Brussel Sprouts

Skulk

Joey & Chris were enjoying some camping and Barbecuing. Little did they know that a sinister bear was skulking right around the corner eying their smores for dinner and them for dessert.

Skulk: out of sight, typically with a sinister or cowardly motive.
    Synonym: Lurk   Antonym: Confront
    Say What? skuhlk   BOM 2

Absolutely Vocabulous — irremediable BOM 3

Clarise and husband Frederick posted more than 100 of these posters in spite of knowing in their heart of hearts the problem was **irremediable**.

irremediable: impossible to cure or put right
Synonym: Irreparable   Say What? ir-re-medi-able   Antonym: Curable

©2020 AbVocab Publishing, Inc. www.facebook.com/abvocab www.abvocab.com AbVocab™ with SketchiToons®

Charisma-Unsuspecting

The **charismatic** used car salesman hid the silver spray pain can as he tried to sell the flood damaged car to an **unsuspecting** customer. "Just a little paint over the chassis job, no biggie".

Charisma: having great personal charm
  Synonym: Allure   Antonym: Dull
  Say What? kr-iz-muh   BOM 2

Unsuspecting: not aware of danger
  Synonym: Trusting   Antonym: Suspicious
  Say What? Un-suhs-pekt-ing   BOM 2

"I'll just spray paint over this rust, hehe works every time."

Unheralded-Bestial

There are quite a few unsung heroes in the world: day care workers, coal miners, the guy that retrieves the ball in the gutter at the bowling alley, etc, but a public school bus driver would take the cake. This unheralded superhero has to drive a big ass yellow piece of metal that hasn't been repaired since 1960, with screaming, really just bestial children, lobbing all sorts of hurtful truth grenades in their direction and can't turn around or properly defend themself.

Unheralded: not recognized
   Synonym: Unnoticed   Antonym: Noticed
   Say What? uhn-her-uh l-did   BOM 2
Bestial: savagely cruel and depraved
   Synonym: Brutal   Antonym: Innocent
   Say What? bes-chuh l   BOM 2

"Chris Farley says I'll turn this damn bus around! That'll end your precious field trip pretty damn quick huh!"

Putative-Punitive

The students who spray-painted "mouse tits" all over the school walls were putatively going to receive a severe consequence that would be punitive from Principal Mousetis.

Putative: supposed
   Synonym: Alleged   Antonym: Proven
   Say What? pyoo-tuh-tiv   BOM 2
Punitive: intended as punishment
   Synonym: Punisment   Antonym: Rewarding
   Say What? pyoo-ni-tiv   BOM 2

"Mouse Tits, Mouse Tits lol, Mr. Mousetis will never catch me."

Indiscriminate

Jake was indiscriminate in his choice of women. He liked them tall, short, plump, slim, old, outgoing, shy & everything in between.

Indiscriminate: done at random
   Synonym: Random   Antonym: Selective
   Say What? in-di-skri-muh-nuht   BOM 3

"I love Girls, Girls, Girls, Girls…

Absolutely Vocabulous alacrity  BOM 2

Promoted to the 'Ben Franklin Hour,' Jayne was sure she could quickly pay off the exorbitant fees to learn the Banana Split. But her new moniker 'Madam alacrity,' emboldened old drunk geezers with their 'bandz a make her dance.' She vowed to quit after a crude cat-call followed her Cross-Ankle Fireman Spin.

subterfuge: a trick to escape something unpleasant; ruse; artifice
Synonym: Liveliness   Say What? uh-lak-ri-tee

©2020 AbVocab Publishing, Inc. www.facebook.com/abvocab   www.abvocab.com AbVocab™ with SketchiToons®

Sophomoric

Dave Q, the sophomoric teen thought it would be funny to moon the Kwik-E-Mart repeatedly to impress his friends. The store owner called the cops and the kid became the first person in history to be permanently banned from that store.

Sophomoric: pretentious or juvenile
    Synonym: Immature   Antonym: Mature
    Say What? saa-fow-maa-rik   BOM 3

"Dude, can you believe I mooned Kwik-E-Mart?"

Exasperate

Don's dangling dingleberries were giving him a dang fit in Disneyworld. Not only did he lose every dime he had to his name but he was exasperated holding hands with his heat exhausted 2 year old twins while trying to make his way to the nearest restroom as he was clenching his butt cheeks because "it" was touching cotton. Talk about a dang emergency!

Exasperate: irritated & frustrated
    Synonym: Agitate   Antonym: Placate
    Say what? uhg-za-spr-eit   BOM 3

Dingleberry: toilet paper clings to anus hairs
Touching Cotton: turd starts poking out, touching the cotton in your underwear

Dang Blasted kids spending all my dang money. Dang dingleberries!

"What a Nightmare. I'm broke & dingleberries causing me a dang fit!"

Blithe

Proton Optimist & neutral Neutron drove to the party in the nucleus. Electron Pessimist who was straight chillin' in the outside orbital didn't want to come. He said "that party is going to suck, I hate being negative but it always does". Proton was so excited to meet some other sub-atoms and was always positive. Neutron was blithe about the whole experience. Eh, whatever happens will happen.

Blithe: cheerful and carefree
    Synonym: Carefree Antonym: Thoughtful
    Say What? blaith   BOM 2

Proton: subatomic particle with a positive electric charge
Electron: subatomic particle with a negative electric charge
Neutron: subatomic particle with a neutral electric charge

Dude, I heard DNA was gonna be at the party in the nucleus tonight! Gonna be lit.

Absolutely Vocabulous — apathetic  BOM 3

Mouse Jeff was completely **apathetic** to finishing the maze after reaching the first 'reward' of crack-cocaine, allowing budding behavioral scientists Alice and Abraham to demonstrate the dangers of drugs to their class.

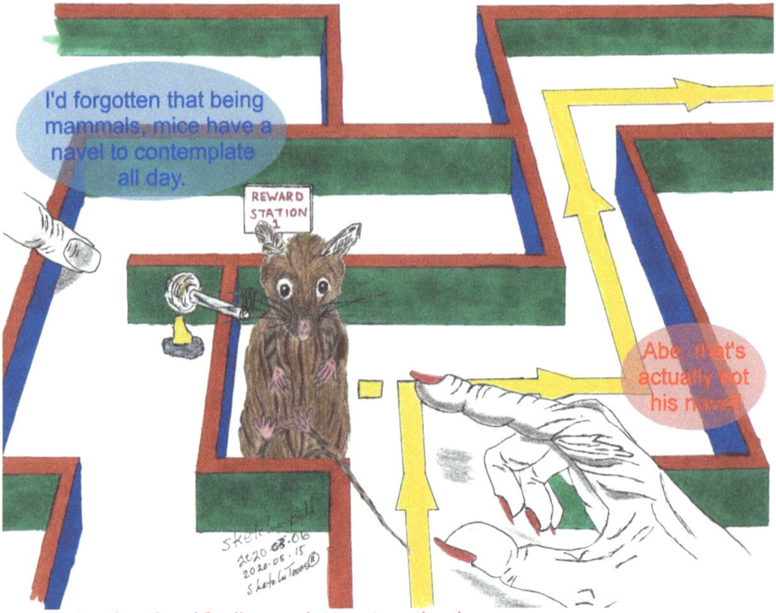

I'd forgotten that being mammals, mice have a navel to contemplate all day.

Abe, that's actually not his navel.

apathetic: showing / feeling no interest, enthusiasm, or concern
Synonym: Indifferent   Say What? ap-uh-thet-ik   Antonym: Responsive

©2020 AbVocab Publishing, Inc. www.facebook.com/abvocab www.abvocab.com AbVocab™ with SketchiToons®

Vain

For this one, I'm just going to quote Kanye West directly. You tell me if this meets the definition of vain.

"God chose me. I am God's vessel. But my greatest pain in life is that I will never be able to see myself perform live." He wouldn't be vain enough to run for President would he? Yep, he sure would.

Vain: having or showing an excessively high opinion of one's appearance, abilities, or worth
   Synonym: Cocky   Antonym: Modest
   Say What? vein   BOM 1

"It's a shame I can't see myself perform live." Wow

50

Querulous-Rectify-Reputable

Poor Pluto. He was on the varsity team of planets for 90 years. Then a group of querulous scientists tried to rectify the situation by demoting him to the JV team. Just like that. No sorry or thank you for not falling out of your axis all those years, nothin'. No longer reputable, Pluto now sits around all day playing Fortnite, complaining & waiting for his day to be pulled back up to the big leagues again.

Querulous: complaining and whining
    Synonym: Grouchy   Antonym: Easy-Going
    Say What? kweh-ruh-luhs   BOM 3

Rectify: put something right; correct
    Synonym: Amend   Antonym: Worsen
    Say What? rek-tuh-fahy   BOM 2

Reputable: having a good reputation
    Synonym: Credible   Antonym: Unscrupulous
    Say What? rep-yuh-tuh-buh l   BOM 2

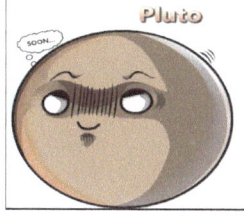

"Reclassification my ass, they are just a bunch of haters"

Absolutely Vocabulous — blasphemous   BOM 3

In spite of four weeks of greatly increased sales from the endorsement, the ad campaign was canceled after a twitter storm labeled the ad **blasphemous**. Miller executive Ava Nuther said: "those folks should just lite'n up."

blasphemous: disrespectful against God or sacred things; sacrilegious
Synonym: Sacrilegious   Say What? blas-fuh-muhs   Antonym: Reverent
©2020 AbVocab Publishing, Inc. www.facebook.com/abvocab   www.abvocab.com   AbVocab™ with SketchiToons®

Remorseful

Superman and Batman had a skirmish. It started when Batman kept hitting on Lois Lane. Superman told him that she was his girl but Batman still flirted with her. So Superman paid him a visit and told him to back off. Superman felt no *remorse* for strangling Batman & Batman felt no contrition for trying to pick up Lois. This was not over.

Remorseful: feel guily or ashamed
    Synonym: Penitent   Antonym: Ruthless
    Say What? ri-mawrs-fuhl   BOM 2

"Lois is my woman, back off!"

Prerequisite

Prerequisites to being an NHL Canadian hockey player include great puck handling skills, knowing how to lay the lumber & extremely poor dental hygiene. Not known for having great salads like their U.S. counterparts, they make up for it by being rough and rugged and possibly just losing another tooth. You will never see them turtling when an opponent drops their gloves & don't ya nowe, they aren't no hosers.

Prerequisite- a thing that is required as a prior condition for something else to happen
    Synonym: Mandate   Antonym: Optional
    Say What? pri-rek-wuh-zit   BOM 2
Lay the Lumber: a slash or hit with the stick
Turtle: crouch down too scared to fight
Salad: beautiful hockey hair

"NHL won't offer me dental insurance."

Hoser: another name for a loser. Before the Zamboni was invented, the losing team had to hose down the ice after the game.

Strenuous

A conspiracy theory suggested that Darth Vader may have had emphysema. Perhaps he was a chain smoker & tar from the cigarettes made its way down his bronchi and eventually blocked his alveoli, those tiny air sacs that allow oxygen to get into his lungs causing strenuous breathing and a disturbing voice?

Strenuous: requiring great exertion
    Synonym: Arduous   Antonym: Easy
    Say What? stren-yoo-uhs   BOM 2
Alveoli: any of the many tiny air sacs of the lungs, which allow for rapid gaseous exchange
Bronchi: any of the major air passages of the lungs which diverge from the windpipe

"I should have listened to my mom and stopped smoking years ago"

Emphysema- a condition in which the air sacs of the lungs are damaged

Absolutely Vocabulous — bombastic — BOM 3

As they awaited entry to the battle place, the drones listened as their leader delivered a **bombastic** tribute to himself.

Yeah Me!!!!!!
Yeah Me!!!!!!
Yeah Me!!!!!!

The ArthOctogon
ENTER ⬇

bombastic: high-sounding but with little meaning; inflated
Synonym: Grandiloquent   Say What? bom-bas-tik   Antonym: Restrained

©2020 AbVocab Publishing, Inc. www.facebook.com/abvocab www.abvocab.com AbVocab™ with SketchiToons®

Jubilant

There are a ton of cool things about Japan so I get the Japanophilia: Geishas, Samurais, mount fuji, cherry blossoms, electric city, sumo wrestling and of course anime and manga. Weeboos get so *jubilant* when they dress up in costumes that passerby's don't know if it is Halloween or a anime convention in town.

Jubilant: feeling or expressing great happiness and triumph

Synonym: Triumphant   Antonym: Sad
Say What? joo-buh-luh-nt   BOM 2

Over-Zealous Weeboos

Weeboo: An overly zealous anime fan

54

Garrulous-Loquacious-Terse

Greta the gossiping garrulous gab & Lorraine the long-winded, loose-lipped loquacious loudmouth went on a double date with Mike the muffled mute & timid & terse Timmy.

Garrulous: talkative
Loquacious: talkative
    Synonym: Chatty   Antomny: Pithy
    Say What? gar-uh-luhs
    Say What? loh-kwey-shuhs   BOM 3
Terse: brief in speech
    Synonym: Pithy   Antonym: Verbose
    Say What? turs   BOM 2

Mike & Timmy can't get a word in with these 2 long winded garrulous gabs

Fortuitous

Have you contemplated how fortuitous that you are to be alive today. 200 million sperm enter the vagina running & ½ will die right away because of the acidity. Another ½ get lost in the wrong fallopian tube. Another ½ are misshapen, have 2 heads or 2 tails or can't swim. Only about 2 million make it into the cervix and even less make it to the egg. So you are one lucky bastard.

Fortuitous: lucky chance
    Synonym: Fortunate   Antonym: Unlucky
    Say What? fawr-too-i-tuhs   BOM 2
Fallopian Tube: pair of tubes along which eggs travel from the ovaries to the uterus.
Cervix: narrow passage into uterus

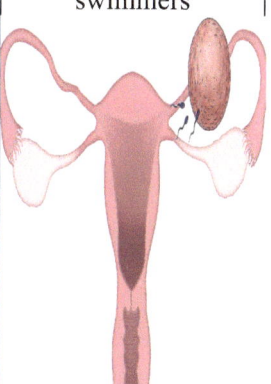

Down to 3 fortuitous swimmers

Flagellum: thin tail that enables swimmming

Dapper

Ron thought he looked dapper so he was baffled when he won the creepiest looking mustache award for the 3rd straight year. "My handlebar stache is straight fire, just hatin'."

Dapper: well-groomed, neat
    Synonym: Debonair   Antonym: Slovenly
    Say What? dap-er   BOM 2

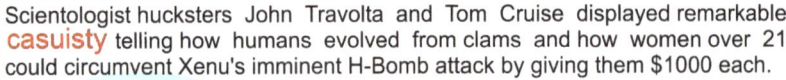

casuisty

Scientologist hucksters John Travolta and Tom Cruise displayed remarkable **casuisty** telling how humans evolved from clams and how women over 21 could circumvent Xenu's imminent H-Bomb attack by giving them $1000 each.

"We'll have more money than Tony Robbins! But, Tom this couch is sort of squishy. Is it the Oprah Couch?"

"Yes, it is John. If only I'd brought my E-meter then. She'd have joined us."

casuistry: use of clever but unsound reasoning; deception
Synonym: Equivocate   Say What? kazh-oo-uh-stree   Antonym: Frankness

©2020 AbVocab Publishing, Inc. www.facebook.com/abvocab   www.abvocab.com   AbVocab™ with SketchiToons®

Dishearten

After 4 failed auditions at the 'Bachelor in Paradise' tv show, Camilla was **disheartened** when the shows producer called and said she was not good enough. She bellied up to the bar and started pounding Mai Tais pondering other options because she did not want to return to her small town a loser and leave paradise.

Dishearten - to depress or ruin one's hopes
  Synonym: Dismay   Antonym: Inspirit
  Say What? dis-hahr-tn   BOM 3

Hmm…there is always waitressing? Pole dancing? Looking for a sugar daddy?

Ignominy

While playing cornhole, Amanda managed to throw her beanbag in the hole on her own board proving to be the best player for the other team. She quit on the spot in ignominy. Nobody knows how she managed to be so bad.

Ignominy: public shame or disgrace
    Synonym: Disgrace   Antonym: Glory
    Say What? ig-nuh-mi-nee   BOM 2

How did I throw the beanbag in my own hole!

Insular

Boujee Bhabie is the undisputed trap queen in Lancelot, real talk. This no nonsense Foxy Cleopatra might seem insular from the surface but she is able to do the dishes, clean the laundry, watch the castle & please her man all the while displaying elite level swag. No cappin'.

Insular: ignorant of or uninterested in cultures, ideas, or peoples outside one's own experience
    Synonym: ignorant   Antonym: cultured
    Say What? in·suh·lr   BOM 2

Boujee: high class female who tends to be ballin' & flossin'

Cappin: frontin' or saying stuff that isn't true

Trap Queen- the baddest female, she is loyal to her friends, lives for her family, and gives no bleeps about bitter, petty bi*ches.

Avarice

Tim & Ava were having an amicable divorce until Ava found out about Tim's off shore bank account. Her avarice when into high gear when she demanded all of the money or else she threatened to take the kids.

Avarice: extreme greed for material gain
    Synonym: Greed   Antonym: Generosity
    Say What? a-vr-uhs   BOM 2

Ava: "It's mine. If you don't give me the money I'm taking the kids!"

57

Absolutely Vocabulous — complacent

The President of Acme Works had earned the distaste of his employees including Jeff. On encountering the president, Jeff thought it was safe to give him a surreptitious 'raspberry.' Unfortunately, Jeff had become **complacent** about using his green coronavirus mask. Unmuffled and big tongue. Exit Jeff.

complacent: overly content with one's achievements or actions
Synonym: Pleased   Say What? kuhm-pley-suhnt   Antonym: Concerned

©2020 AbVocab Publishing, Inc. www.facebook.com/abvocab www.abvocab.com AbVocab™ with SketchiToons®

Charlatan

The crackpot charlatan got rejected to sell his enlargement pills on any prime time infomercial so he took his hardware door to door. He was mainly met with cold shoulders & menacing glares. There were a few desperate young men that wanted to know more.

Charlatan: a person falsely claiming to have a special knowledge or skill; a fraud
   Synonym: Swindler   Antonym: Honesty
   Say What? shaar-luh-tn   BOM 3

"So, my product works 100% of the time, some of the time. Buy 1 & get the 2nd full price."

58

Pungent

All of the stories the mother heard from other mom's about what happens during puberty, could not prepare her for the werewolf that her little Timmy was becoming. She couldn't believe that his tiny pituitary gland would cause what he turned into. He was now a broad shouldered, 5 o'clock shadowed, deep voiced, loose sacked, pungent smelling, acne infested, mood swinging hornball.

Pungent: having a strong taste or smell
    Synonym: Acrid   Antonym: Bland
    Say What? puhn-jnt   BOM 2

Pituitary Gland: small pea-sized gland that secretes human growth hormone during puberty

My mom says my pits are pungent.

Puberty- the period during which adolescents reach sexual maturity

Lascivious

The male peacock had vivid rainbow feathers that he revealed in a lascivious manner to all the female peahens surrounding him. "Yea, that's right ladies, you see what I got going on."

Lascivious: showing an overt and often offensive sexual desire
    Synonym: Sensual   Antonym: Chaste
    Say What? luh-si-vee-uhs   BOM 3

"See those shiny feathers girls? There's more where that came from."

Serendipity

Captain Jolly had been searching for years for treasure and always came up empty. That was before he experienced the most serendipitous discovery of his life. "Ahhh shiiit, we going to Vegas"!

Serendipity: the occurrence and development by chance in a happy or beneficial way
    Synonym: Luck   Antonym: Misfortune
    Say What? ser-uhn-dip-itee   BOM 3

Aye, Blimey! Plunder de booty.

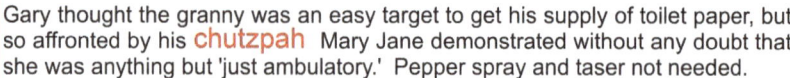 

chutzpah   BOM 3

Gary thought the granny was an easy target to get his supply of toilet paper, but so affronted by his **chutzpah** Mary Jane demonstrated without any doubt that she was anything but 'just ambulatory.' Pepper spray and taser not needed.

chutzpah: shameless audacity; impudence
Synonym: Gall   Say What? hoo-t-spuh   Antonym: Meek
©2020 AbVocab Publishing, Inc. www.facebook.com/abvocab   www.abvocab.com   AbVocab™ with SketchiToons®

Evasive

The boss was evasive when confronted by workers who wanted a raise. "Depending on the circumstances, if sales increase next year, some people may receive a tiny pay increase if they have worked here longer than 20 years and haven't missed work in 3 years and if they are in the top 4 people in sales but that is not guaranteed."

Evasive: deceitful, trickery
  Synonym: Cagey   Antonym: Forthright
  Say What? uh-vei-suhv   BOM 2

My boss said I may get a raise, but don't ask him and don't show up at his office. Hmmmmm.

Conundrum-Narcissistic-Ogle

The disproportionately built weightlifter had extremely large biceps, triceps & chest making it a conundrum how his toothpick legs could support his top heavy frame. As he strutted around narcissistically oogling at himself in the mirror, he would tell anyone within earshot of him "bi's and tri's day".

Conundrum: a confusing and difficult problem or question
    Synonym: Riddle
    Say What? kuh-nuhn-druhm   BOM 2

Narcissistic: having an excessive interest in oneself and one's physical appearance
    Synonym: Conceited   Antonym: Unselfish
    Say What? naar-suh-si-stuhk   BOM 3

Ogle: stare at in a sensual manner
    Synonym: Gawk   Antonym: Ignore
    Say What? ow-gl   BOM 2

"Look at these guns. Bi's and Tri's day. After I eat this protein bar, doing more dumbell curls."

Amorous

Brendan had amorous thoughts about robots and was considering ordering one online. Agalmatophilia was something he wondered if ran in the family as he remembered his uncle always acting peculiar around the vacuum.

Amorous: strong feelings of love
    Synonym: Erotic   Antonym: Invidious
    Say What? a-mr-uhs   BOM 2

Agalmatophilia: attraction to an robot

Something very strange going on

Luminary

Lionel Messi is the world famous Argentinian soccer luminary. Even though only 5'9" tall, Lionel has a skill set that is unmatched.

Luminary: a star who influences others
    Synonym: Celebrity   Antonym: Nobody
    Say What? loo-muh-ner-ee   BOM 2

Absolutely Vocabulous — condemn BOM 3

Seeking to undo widespread **condemnation** of the Mullet, Tennis Star Andre Agassi took to the late night circuit to promote "National Mullet Day." He lauded the Kentucky waterfall, yep-nope and reminded that only his Tennessee Top Hat was memorable about President Polk. Not sublime. Not a 'white trash do.'

So, folks July 2nd is your day to flaunt that Mississippi Mud Flap. I'll be with you in spirit.

You Finally have it National Mullet Day.

condemn: express complete disapproval of, typically in public
Synonym: Reproach   Say What? kon-dem-ney-shuhn   Antonym: Endorsement
©2020 AbVocab Publishing, Inc. www.facebook.com/abvocab www.abvocab.com AbVocab™ with SketchiToons®

Anagram	Examples

Anagram: a word or phrase formed by rearranging the letters of a different word or phrase, using all the letters exactly once
    Synonym: Scrabble
    Say What? an-uh-gram   BOM 2
	Dormitory = Dirty Room
	
	Justin Timberlake = I'm A Jerk But Listen

Salacious-Blemish-Lambaste

Jared couldn't believe the pickle he was in. He was the little league coach for his son's baseball team. Last practice, while talking to the team mom Becky, who many thought was salacious coquette, a kid hit a pearod directly into his neck. As a result, it left a blemish that looked suspiciously identical to a hickey. When he got home his wife Suzie lambasted him "You bastard! It's Becky isn't it. That little homewrecker".

Gulp, well this is going to be a tough one to explain on the home front. Peadrod to the neck.

Salacious: inappropriate interest in sex
    Synonym: Erotic   Antonym: Pure
    Say What? sah-lei-shuhs   BOM 3

Blemish: a small mark or flaw that ruins the appearance of something
    Synonym: Defect   Antonym: Perfection
    Say What? blem-ish   BOM 2

Lambaste: criticize sharply
    Synonym: Castigate   Antonym: Praise
    Say What? lam-beist   BOM 2

Pearod- A hard line drive batted back at the pitcher

Coquette- a flirty woman

Virulent

Would you rather be suffocated by an anaconda constrictor snake or be bit by an inland taipan, the most virulent snake in the world which causes slurred speech, seizures, difficulty breathing & internal bleeding?

Virulent: a disease or poison extremely severe or harmful
    Synonym: Noxious   Antonym: Harmless
    Say What? vir-yuh-luhnt   BOM 2

Absolutely Vocabulous conjecture BOM 3

A credit charge listed as 'Equine Research Fund' caused Lucille to **conjecture** that husband Clem got nothing from his Gambler's Anonymous meetings. The missent text made it a certainty. Dispute the Charge? Cancel the Card!

 Thks Jmy D Grk. Great Pick!

Look at that powerful rump. Put $5 Grand on the nose at 14 to 1. Dead Cert!! Champagne on me!

 Direct to the biggest Horse's Ass. u r busted. Dead for cert!

conjecture: an opinion or conclusion formed on the basis of incomplete info
Synonym:Surmise   Say What?Kuhn-jek-cher   Antonym:Proof
©2020 AbVocab Publishing, Inc. www.facebook.com/abvocab   www.abvocab.com   AbVocab™ with SketchiToons®

Presage

Having a lot of unprotected sexual encounters, although fun & adventurous, can **presage** trouble. On the mild end is crabs on your pubic hair & next thing you know you are in the Walgreens medical isle looking for that special shampoo. On the severe end, Herpes, aka the gift that keeps on giving, will make you never want to look at another person again.

Presage: a sign or warning that something
　　Synonym: Foretell　　Antonym: Conceal
　　Say What? pri-seyj　　　　　　BOM 2

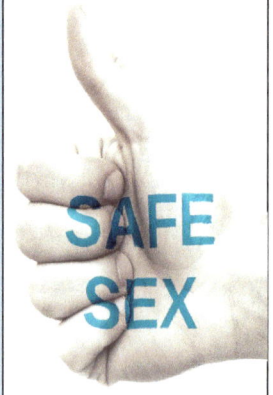

64

Highbrow-Connoisseur

Pierre is not usually picky about anything except for coffee, but man does he become highbrow all of a sudden. He will tell you that it has to be pure Kona beans directly from Kona, Hawaii because of the perfect microclimate with volcanic soil & rain & sun. If another pretend connoisseur offers their take on the best coffee, Pierre quickly shuts them down, "nope, not better than Kona".

Highbrow: scholarly or rarefied in taste
    Synonym: Scholarly   Antonym: Uncultured
    Say What? hai-braw   BOM 2

Connoisseur: expert judge in matters of taste
    Synonym: Aficionado Antonym: Ignoramus
    Say What? kaa-nuh-sur   BOM 3

I love me some Kona Coffee!

Microclimate- climate of a very small or restricted area.

Glutton

As I sat on the couch watching the gluttonous Mukbang youtuber shoving crab legs, sushi rolls & lobster tails in her mouth I couldn't help but wonder why this was so fascinating but also, does that Japanese restaurant down the street deliver at 1 AM?

Glutton: an excessively greedy eater
    Synonym: Gorger   Antonym: Abstemious
    Say What? gluht-n   BOM 2

Mukbang- an online audiovisual food broadcast

Now I want to order sushi

Rudimentary

Sensei Sakura was trying to teach a rudimentary kata to his student but was growing frustrated because the student could not get it. "I said uke (block) not Zuki (punch), forget it, let's just pick up again next class".

Rudimentary: most basic form
    Synonym: Elemental   Antonym: Complex
    Say What? roo-duh-men-tuh-ree   BOM 2

Kime! (focus)

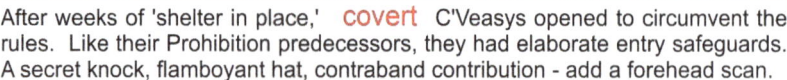

covert

After weeks of 'shelter in place,' **covert** C'Veasys opened to circumvent the rules. Like their Prohibition predecessors, they had elaborate entry safeguards. A secret knock, flamboyant hat, contraband contribution - add a forehead scan.

covert: not openly acknowledged or displayed
Synonym: Clandestine   Say What? koh-vert   Antonym: Revealed

©2020 AbVocab Publishing, Inc. www.facebook.com/abvocab   www.abvocab.com   AbVocab™ with SketchiToons®

Melodramatic

The spoiled 16 year old girl was being so **melodramatic** because her parents bought her a used Honda when she got her license. "ughhh, like this is the worst ever, I thought I was going to get a brand new Mercedes. What will I tell my friends?"

Melodramatic: exaggerated, sensationalized, or overemotional with small things

Synonym: Theatrical   Antonym: Calm
Say What? mel-uh-druh-mat-ik   BOM 2

OMG, like, I wanted a Mercedes

Maven-Unkempt

Kelly, the undisputed surfing maven, was stoked to be out on dawn patrol off the coast of Portugal. He was a big Kahuna riding gnarly waves while staying unkempt in appearance. Kelly snaked his way out and saw a monster tsunami wave. He turtle rolled to catch the barrel of the wave. This wave was 60 feet high! He tried to hang ten and realized he was losing control. "Oh, Shiiiit, I'm about to wipeout".

Maven: an expert
    Synonym: Connoisseur   Synonym: Novice
    Say What? mei-vn   BOM 2
Unkempt: Unclean appearance
    Synonym: Bedraggled   Synonym: Dapper
    Say What? uhn-kempt   BOM 2

"Bruh, I don't know how I'm still alive, major wipe out on that bitchin' wave"

Turtle Roll- the surfer flips the board over in front of an oncoming wave

Haughty-Imperious

In the early 1800's, the haughty settlers moved West plowing over the Natives, nearly killing off the buffalo in the process, in search of Gold & free land under the banner of the imperious sounding 'Manifest Destiny'.

Haughty: arrogantly superior
    Synonym: Arrogant   Antonym: Meek
    Say What? haa-tee   BOM 2
Imperious: assuming power or authority without justification
    Synonym: Domineering   Antonym: Servile
    Say What? uhm-pee-ree-uhs   BOM 3
Manifest Destiny: belief in the US that its settlers were destined to expand.

"Move over Natives, we were here first. Wait, no we weren't but either way, ya'll gotta move"

Prodigy

Kyrie Irving is a basketball prodigy. Sick crossovers, pull up J's, rock handling wizardry, he's got defenders on skates.

Prodigy: a young person exceptionally talented
    Synonym: Wunderkind Antonym: Mediocre
    Say What? praa-duh-jee   BOM 2

Kyrie getting ankles

Absolutely Vocabulous **ephemeral** BOM 3

On their anniversary, Ted lined up petals toward a bouquet by the bed hoping he would get luck that night. Unfortunately, his efforts proved **ephemeral** when he lit the fireworks before the party had even started.

You've go to be kidding. Let's just watch Netflix and chill.

ephemeral: lasting only a very short time.
Synonym: Fleeting   Say What? ih-fem-er-uhl   Ant: Enduring

©2020 AbVocab Publishing, Inc. www.facebook.com/abvocab   www.abvocab.com AbVocab™ with SketchiToons®

Jest

I told Jaden his momma is so hairy, she shaves with a weed-whacker in *jest* not knowing that his mom actually suffered from hypertrichosis. This condition is so rare I mean what are the chances?

Jest: a thing said or done for amusement
 Synonym: Joke   Antonym: Serious
 Say What? jest   BOM 2

Hypertrichosis: aka werewolf syndrome, is a condition characterized by a shit ton of hair

"Oh, sorry dude, my bad."

Pic of Jaden's Mom

Viscosity-Turgid

Fred the frog was excited "I see fly, ooooh, supper". Watch. In .07 seconds, Fred shot his tongue out and the dragonfly was a goner. If humans had a tongue like frogs it would stretch to our bellybutton. With reversible saliva, Fred changes the viscosity so it can latch on to the dragonfly and then dissolve it. Turgid and full of energy, Fred is back to chirping the night away.

Viscosity: thickness of fluid
   Synonym: Thickness
   Say What? vi-skos-i-tee
Turgid: swollen and distended or congested
   Synonym: Swollen   Antonym: Thin
   Say What? turjid   BOM 2

"You don't stand a chance dragonfly! I got super power saliva bitches"

Reversible Saliva- thick and sticky during prey capture, then turns thin and watery as prey is removed

Creed

Jebediah, an Amish teenager, was living it up during Rumspringa. He went dancing, smoked a cigar & kissed a girl. He was debating the pro's and con's in his mind about returning home. The con's had to do with the Amish creed of no technology, music or pictures. On the pro side, he had come to really enjoy the simple life. The deal breaker for him came when he started thinking about the cinnamon rolls. Oh I am never leaving he finally thought.

Creed: to belief in or acceptance of something as true
   Synonym: Doctrine   Antonym: Doubt
   Say What? kreed   BOM 2
Rumspringa: rite of passage during adolescence in Amish culture

Who needs modern vehicles tbh when you can eat those cinnamon rolls!

Amish- Swiss & German Christians. known for simple living, plain dress, and reluctance to use modern technology.

Absolutely Vocabulous — irreverent

If the sketches in their book are too *irreverent* or too sophisticated to share with all your friends and neighbors, the authors at least ensure you that all the defined words are, in fact, bona fide words. Well, not those catawampus ones.

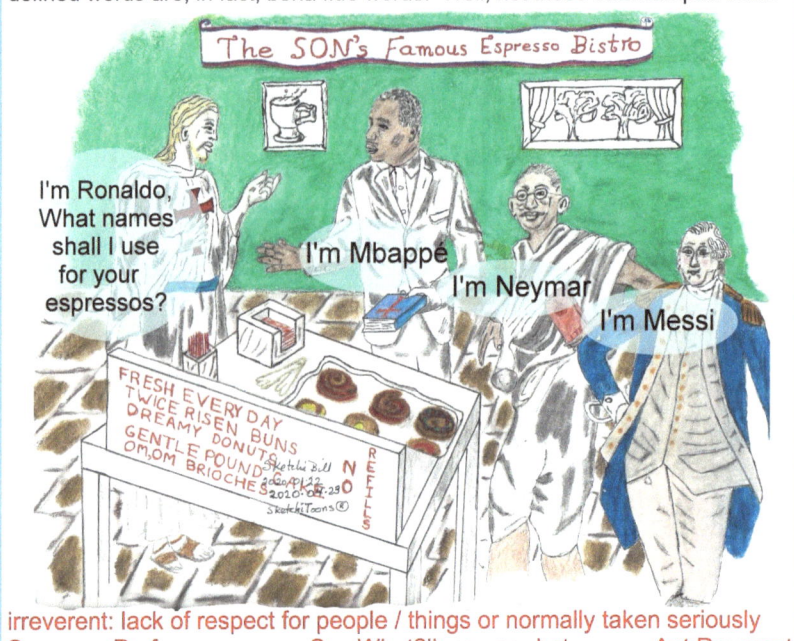

irreverent: lack of respect for people / things or normally taken seriously
Synonym: Profane   Say What? ih-rev-er-uhnt   Ant: Reverent

©2020 AbVocab Publishing, Inc. www.facebook.com/abvocab   www.abvocab.com AbVocab™ with SketchiToons®

Quibble

Bacon is delicious. This is a fact. One shouldn't *quibble* over trivial matters like saturated fat levels causing high cholesterol possibly leading to stroke, heart disease & diabetes. I mean come on, it's delicious! #sarcasm

Quibble: a slight objection or criticism about a trivial matter

Synonym: Object   Antonym: Approve
Say What? kwi-bl   BOM 2

Bacon is so delicious it may be worth the heart problems

Seditious-Proletariat

The Beavers were building dams for an oligarchic ruling class that ruled the river with an iron fist. Rumblings of sedition starting to emerge from the proletariat class of beavers. Che, a vocal leader of the working class spoke up "all we do is work all day to find food and build damn dams for the elite while they sunbathe. Hells to the no, today that changes. Who want to stage a coup with me? At sundown tonight, we revolt".

Seditious: rebel against authority
    Synonym: Mutinous   Antonym: Calm
    Say What? si-dish-uh s   BOM 2

Proletariat: working-class people
    Synonym: Commoner Antonym: Aristrocrat
    Say What? proh-li-tair-ee-uht   BOM 3

At sundown we rise up

Coup D'etat: removal of a government from power by force

Oligarchy: a small group of people ruling a country

Atrophy-Loathe

Tad had been working as a Federal IT employee for 20 years. He spent most of his day playing Candy Crush & checking to see if the copy machine was fixed. His hair was thinning & his muscular physique had atrophied into flab. He loathed the thought of doing this for the next 15 years just to get the chance to grow old.

Atrophy: muscle becomes fat
    Synonym: Degeneration   Antonym: Grow
    Say What? a-truh-fee   BOM 2

Loathe: intense hatred
    Synonym: Hate   Antonym: Love
    Say What? lowth   BOM 2

"I guess I'll play another 4 hours of Candy Crush, nobody seems to notice. I loathe this job."

Finesse

Roger Federer turns tennis into art. He mixes finesse & grace with strength & power making him unstoppable on grass, clay or hard courts.

Finesse: intricate & refined delicacy
    Synonym: Grace   Antonym: Clumsy
    Say What? fi-ness   BOM 1

Absolutely Vocabulous — sedentary

The doctor's attempts to inculcate John the fact that his **sedentary** lifestyle put him at risk of diabetes and more was unsuccessful until John required oxygen assist. John immediately got off the couch - and perhaps he will soon join with the kids and relive his glory days of soccer.

sedentary: tending to spend too much time without moving
Synonym: Inactive   Say What? sed-n-ter-ee   Antonym: Mobile
©2020 AbVocab Publishing, Inc. www.facebook.com/abvocab   www.abvocab.com   AbVocab™ with SketchiToons®

Exhort

I strongly **exhort** people not to text and drive. You may think you are just glancing at your phone but your brain is getting sucked into a deep dark abyss & the road and other cars won't wait for you to come out of it. In case you don't know, that text you are sending is really not that important.

Exhort: to strongly encourage or urge someone to do something
    Synonym: Beseech   Antonym: Dissuade
    Say What? ig-zawrt   BOM 2

Hey dumbass, put the phone down. Your text is not that important and you are going to kill someone. End of message.

72

Antagonist-Mediator

Brock the biceps & triceps Trey couldn't stand each other. The problem was both wanted to be huge and noticed. Being antagonistic, if one flexed the other extended. Henry the Humerus wanted to be funny but couldn't laugh when caught up in the middle of these 2 meatheads. He tried to mediate but it was pointless. So he just cracked jokes to himself and ignored them.

Mediator: a person who resolves a conflict
    Synonym: Referee   Antonym: Fighter
    Say What? mee-dee-ey-ter   BOM 2

Antagonist: to actively oppose something
    Synonym: Adversary   Antonym: Friend
Say What? an-tag-uh-nist   BOM 2

See me? I'm that thin, hilarious little bone in between those 2 idiots.

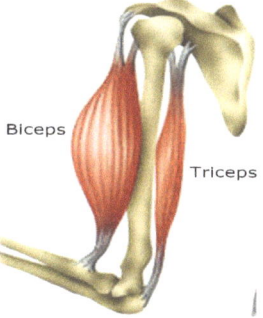

Humerus- the long bone in the upper arm.

Upend-Orthodoxy

Suffragist reformers Elizabeth Cady Stanton, Sojourner Truth & Susan B Anthony were pissed when they tried to upend the prevailing orthodoxy of the day. Oh hell no, this is some bs they thought, so you're telling me that women, who make up ½ of the population, multi-task better than men, reproduce, take care of children, are emotionally intelligent, more articulate and have better style, can't vote!

Upend: to overthrow
    Synonym: Overturn   Antonym: Keep
    Say What? uhp-end   BOM 2

Orthodoxy: generally accepted theory, doctrine, or practice
    Synonym: Doctrine   Antonym: Disbelief
    Say What? or-thuh-daak-see   BOM 2

I demand my flippin voting rights!

Suffrage- the right to vote. Women could finally vote in the US in 1920 with the 19th Amendment.

Absolutely Vocabulous — segregate  BOM 2

Segregated from the prokaryotes and viruses because of their elite attitude, the eukaryotes were still throwing shade and intimidating the others. Just having a nucleus and mitochondria is no reason to put fellow students down.

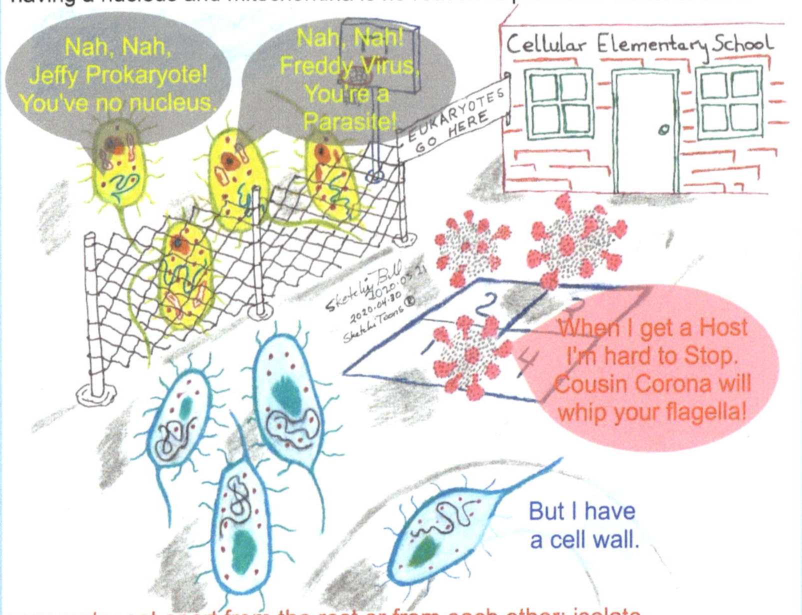

Nah, Nah, Jeffy Prokaryote! You've no nucleus.

Nah, Nah! Freddy Virus, You're a Parasite!

Cellular Elementary School

EUKARYOTES GO HERE

When I get a Host I'm hard to Stop. Cousin Corona will whip your flagella!

But I have a cell wall.

segregate: set apart from the rest or from each other; isolate
Synonym: Separate   **Say What?** seg-ri-gey-tid   **Antonym:** Unite

©2020 AbVocab Publishing, Inc. www.facebook.com/abvocab   www.abvocab.com   AbVocab™ with SketchiToons®

Ramification-Cirrhosis

The man's liver had finally had enough. The **ramification** of pounding hard liquor & wine for years had finally reached its end. His liver became hardened and developed **cirrhosis**.

Ramification: a consequence of an action or event, usually unwelcome
   Synonym: Repercussion   Antonym: Cause
   Say What? ram-uh-fi-key-shuhn   BOM 2

Cirrhosis: the liver does not function properly due to long-term damage, usually from alcohol

Anathema-Contemptuously

The Duke Blue Devil men's basketball team surpasses the Yankees, Cowboys, Notre Dame football & the Patriots as the biggest anathema in sports. What is so repelling? Well first, we can start with Coach K, who UNC fans contemptuously call vicious little ferret. Refs dare not upset him as he browbeats them from the sideline. He also happens to be the best coach of all time, to be fair. Second, Dick Vitale is obnoxious in his favoritism of Duke. Third is a combination of getting calls, flopping & dirty play.

Browbeat- intimidate someone with stern or abusive words (what coach K does regularly).

Anathema: something that is hated
    Synonym: Pariah   Antonym: Loved
    Say What? uh-nath-uh-muh   BOM 3

Contemptuous: feeling that someone or something is beneath consideration
    Synonym: Scornful   Antonym: Flattering
    Say What? kuhn-temp-choo-uhs   BOM 3

Supercilious-Ebullient-Neophyte

The teenage mutant ninja turtles are a supercilious bunch. They strut around with their shells perfectly polished, vivid colored headbands & ebullient personalities. But, neophytes they are not with the nun chucks.

Supercilious: acting superior to others
    Synonym: Arrogant   Antonym: Humble
    Say What? soo-pr-si-lee-uhs   BOM 3

Ebullient: cheerful and full of energy
    Synonym: Chipper   Antonym: Sad
    Say What? ih-buhl-yuh-nt   BOM 3

Neophyte: Beginner
    Synonym: Greenhorn   Antonym: Expert
    Say What? nee-uh-fahyt   BOM 3

These heroes in a half shell may be supercilious but not neophytes.

Absolutely Vocabulous: self-deprecating

After five months as a Concert Promoter, **self-deprecating** Gemma came to the realization that with her skill set and temperament, she would surely starve unless she found a new profession. Law school? Med school?

At least there is no waiting!

self-deprecating: overly modest or critical of oneself, especially with humor
Synonym: belittle   Say What? self-dep-ri-keyt   Antonym: commend

©2020 AbVocab Publishing, Inc. www.facebook.com/abvocab www.abvocab.com AbVocab™ with SketchiToons®

Badinage

The two teenagers smacked each other and laughed going back and forth calling each other names in playful **badinage** more commonly called flirting.

Badinage: humorous or playful
  Synonym: Banter   Antonym: Serious
  Say What? bad-n-ij   BOM 2

Foray

You may have never heard of the Candiru parasite but a few poor souls who had the idea of peeing in the Amazon River sure have. While relieving themselves in the water, the ammonia smell from the urine attracts the parasite. The parasite forays into the urethra of the penis latching onto the walls with barbs. Removal can be very difficult, as the barbs face one direction only, and pulling on the fish only causes them to sink deeper into the walls of the urethra.

Nooooo, Don't Pee in the River!

Foray: an attack into enemy territory
   Synonym: Raid   Antonym: Idleness
   Say What? faw-rei   BOM 2
Urethra: the duct by which urine is conveyed out of the body from the bladder, and which in male vertebrates also conveys semen.

Candiru- aka toothpick fish, or vampire fish, is a species of parasitic freshwater catfish native to the Amazon Basin

Lament-Procure

There was a problem. It was only 10 PM and the keg was tapped out. The party was just getting lit and now it was dried up. All of the carousers lamented that the party might be over. As it's always darkest before the dawn, a hero rose up in the midst of this disaster. A guy knew a guy who had a cousin who kept fresh kegs in his cellar so after a quick call, the keg was procured, game on.

Keg tapped out during party is unforgivable. Thankfully, a new keg was procured.

Lament: a passionate expression of grief
   Synonym: Mourn   Antonym: Celebrate
   Say What? luh-ment   BOM 2
Procure: to get by special effort
   Synonym: Obtain   Antonym: Forfeit
   Say What? proh-kyoor   BOM 2
Carouse: drink alcohol and party hard

Absolutely Vocabulous — smug

When she saw Janet's **smug** look, her mom knew that the vegetarian cat had just gotten a plateful of the greenest peas for supper. Janet's older brother Jeff watched happily as his mom 'fixed her wagon.'

smug: having or showing an excessive pride in oneself or one's achievements
Synonym: Self-Satisfied   Say What? smuhg   Antonym: Unsure

©2020 AbVocab Publishing, Inc. www.facebook.com/abvocab www.abvocab.com AbVocab™ with SketchiToons®

Lampoon

Brock thought it would be funny to lampoon his boss on facebook as an incompetent clown. He soon found himself looking for new employment on job fairs. Lesson: watch who you throw shade at on social media.

Lampoon: publicly criticize someone or something by using ridicule, irony, or sarcasm
    Synonym: Satirize   Antonym: Flatter
    Say What? lam-poon   BOM 2

Apparently the boss didn't think this was funny and now I'm looking for a new job.

Euphemism

Bloodsucking swamp devils, who sometimes go by the euphemism mosquitos, are really just awful little things that have caused more death and misery than anything else ever to live. In fact, when you combine malaria, west nile virus, dengue fever, zika, chikungunya and so on, mosquitoes have killed 5% of everyone who has ever lived! I don't give a mosquito's ass about what happens to the food chain after killing them, **gene edit** those bastards off the planet!

Euphemism: a milder substitute for a word considered to be too harsh
    Synonym: Softening   Antonym: Pejorative
    Say What? yoo-fuh-miz-uh m   BOM 2

Gene Edit these bloodsucking swamp devils

Gene Edit- type of genetic engineering in which DNA is modified

Masochism-Bungling

The Cleveland Browns go down as the worst sports team of the last decade. Yes, I mean any sports team, not just football. They won a craptastic 26% of their games and went through 6 head coaches just to screw the badger. The masochism displayed by bungling one draft pick after another blows the mind. To be this bad, you need a combination of injuries, bad draft picks, terrible luck, more injuries and probably some players gambling against their own team.

Masochism: to derive pleasure from one's own pain or humiliation
    Synonym: Flagellation   Antonym: Sadism
    Say What? ma-suh-ki-zm   BOM 2
Bungle: to carry out a task incompetently
    Synonym: Botch   Antonym: Fix
    Say What? buhng-guhl   BOM 2

No helping these sucky Browns.

Suckage- the amount something sucks. The Browns set the bar so high that no future team could match that level of awfulness.

Absolutely Vocabulous: subterfuge  BOM 3

The man dreaded the 4 stressful meetings scheduled for the day so he practiced some *subterfuge* by professing to his boss to be deathly ill. But, he actually spent all day drinking martinis and watching sports at the pub.

> If my phone rings, please answer it. I'm too sick to come to the phone!
>
> With Pleasure, Sir.
>
> I'll Have Another Double Please.
>
> Absolut-ly!
>
> How about switching to the Hockey Game.
>
> Go Canucks!

subterfuge: a trick to escape something unpleasant; ruse; artifice
Synonym: Ruse   Say What? suhb-ter-fyooj   Antonym: Honesty

©2020 AbVocab Publishing, Inc. www.facebook.com/abvocab www.abvocab.com AbVocab™ with SketchiToons®

Anachronism

In this anachronism, the Spartans checked in their luggage at the airport and flew to the first battle. Before the first battle, the warriors went on twitter to hastag some memes while getting their grenades and machine guns ready.

Anachronism: a thing belonging or appropriate to a period other than that in which it exists
Synonym: Postdate   Antonym: Predate
Say What? ah-na-kruh-ni-zm   BOM 3

Implore

If you are thinking of trying Crystal Meth, I implore you to reconsider. Sure you will get high as a kite as it will target dopamine neurotransmitters in your brain that reward you. But is it worth paranoia, anxiety, mood swings, meth mouth AKA rotting teeth, sores, pimples & premature aging when you look in a mirror and see a Ghoul? Don't do drugs mhm-kay.

Implore: beg someone
    Synonym: Beeseech   Antonym: Refuse
    Say What? im-plawr   BOM 2
Dopamine: compound present in the body as a neurotransmitter; rewards user with a high

Crystal Meth: highly addictive drug that affects the central nervous system causing ghoul-like symptoms

Mien-Piquant-Belie

Henry entered the 20 annual 10 round Spicy Chicken Wing contest. He was looking wobbly by the 8th round but kept battling. The mien on his face got scary after the 9th wing. He was becoming more and more pale. After the 10th wing, the most piquant, he was done. He tried to belie the pain and put on a brave face but that only made him look like some creepy ventriloquist doll.

Henry after the 9th wing.

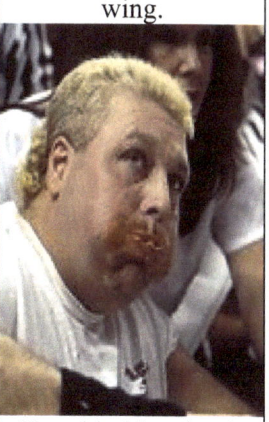

Uggghh, his mien is getting wobbly. He's trying to belie the pain but he is clearly at the end of his rope.

Mien: a person's look or manner
    Synonym: Look   Antonym: Personality
    Say What? meen   BOM 2
Piquant: having a pleasantly sharp taste
    Synonym: Zesty   Antonym: Mild
    Say What? pee-kahnt   BOM 2
Belie: a fake appearance
    Synonym: Distort   Antonym: Authentic
    Say What? bih-lahy   BOM 2

Absolutely Vocabulous: vacuous   BOM 2

Vacuous John and ditzy Joan's marathon date ended abruptly when Joan erroneously texted John instead of her BFF, causing him to shank a last second PAT, costing him entry into the Madden 2021 Finals.

Oh, Shit I texted John not BFF Shirley

Damn you Joan. WTF calling me! Made me shank the winning kick!

vacuous: having or showing a lack of thought or intelligence
Synonym: Dull   Say What? vak-yoo-uhs   Antonym: Intelligent
©2020 AbVocab Publishing, Inc. www.facebook.com/abvocab   www.abvocab.com AbVocab™ with SketchiToons®

Hyperbole

When Joe said if I don't get an A on this test, my mom will kill me, we assumed it was hyperbole. We found out later that some of Joe's family was mysteriously missing and his mom had a lengthy record of assaults.

Hyperbole: exaggerated statements
  Synonym: Exaggerate Antonym: Understate
  Say What? hahy-pur-buh-lee   BOM 2

No Hyperbole, She Crazy

Ostracized-Vindictive-Cantankerous

Daniel Larusso is the teenage boy who plays the protagonist in the movie 'The Karate Kid'. Daniel is ostracized at his new school and bullied. So he learns Karate from Mr. Miyagi, the old Japanese martial arts wizard. Daniel must prepare to face Johnny & the vindictive Cobra Kai dojo led by cantankerous sensei John Kreese. Daniel falls for Ali who is probably way out of his league but he manages to woo her anyway. The movie ends when Daniel defeats Johnny in a tournament with a very sus crane kick that more than likely would have not worked in real life.

Protagonist Daniel with the wizard Mr. Miyagi

Ostracize: to exclude someone from a group
　　Synonym: Blackball　　Antonym: Include
　　Say What? aa-struh-saiz　　　　BOM 2

Protagonist- the leading character

Vindictive: wanting revenge
　　Synonym: Resentful　　Antonym: Forgiving
　　Say What? vuhn-dik-tuhv　　　　BOM 2

Cantankerous: bad-tempered; argumentative
　　Synonym: Crabby　　Antonym: Pleasant
　　Say What? kan-tang-kr-uhs　　　BOM 2

No way Daniel pulls Ali

Disseminate-Promulgate

Man, you aught to hear what comes out of Kayla's mouth. She is a trash talking, FUD disseminating, lip smacking, gossip mongering, bs promulgating windbag who's always keeping someone's name in her mouth.

Kayla disseminating FUD & promulgating bs

Disseminate: to spread information widely
　　Synonym: Propagate　　Antonym: Conceal
　　Say What? dih-sem-uh-neyt　　　BOM 2

Promulgate: to promote or make known
　　Synonym: Spread　　Antonym: Withhold
　　Say What? prom-uhl-geyt　　　　BOM 2

FUD- fear, uncertainty and doubt

Remember, you are intelligent, erudite, imaginative, perceptive, sagacious, resourceful, inquisitive, discerning & knowledgeable.

You are going to Crush that Test!

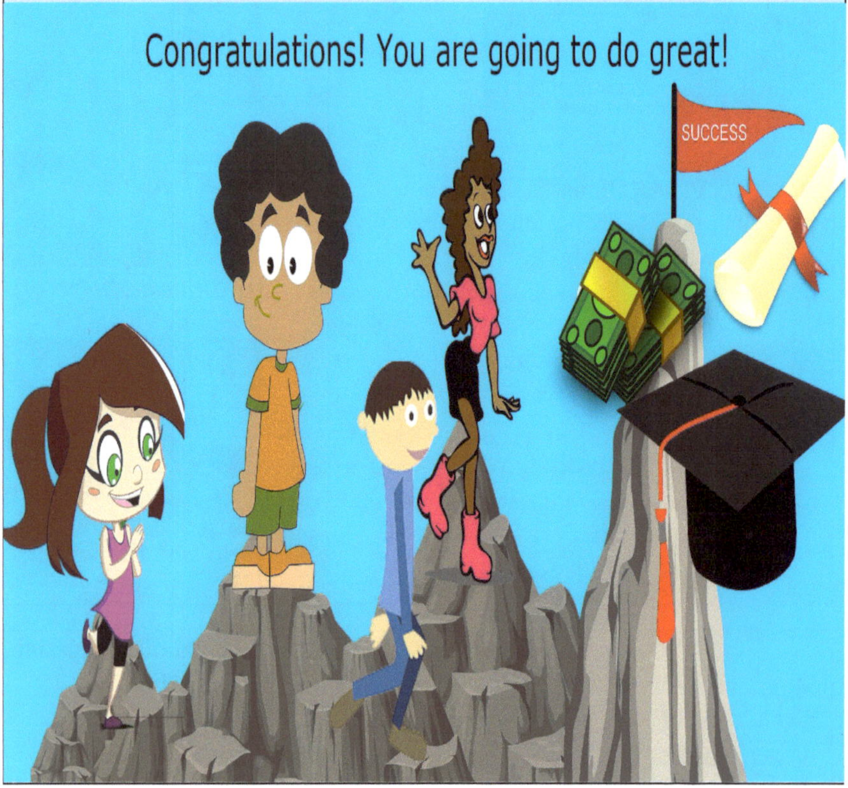
Congratulations! You are going to do great!
SUCCESS

Vocabulous Throwdown is a:

An Absolutely Vocabulous™ Production

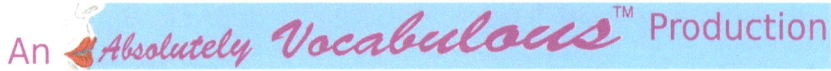

Purchase Vocabulous Throwdown Volume 2 at Amazon.com
to get the entire vocabulous experience

Vocabulary Words for Book (Alphabetical)

Abdicate: to fail to fulfill responsibilities
Acerbic: forthright way of speaking
Adroit: skillfull using the hands or mind
Agalmatophilia: sexual attraction to an inanimate object
Alacrity: brisk and cheerful readiness
Alliteration- using the same letter or sound at the beginning of each word in a sentence
Aloof: distant, remote
Alveoli: any of the many tiny air sacs of the lungs, which allow for rapid gaseous exchange
Amorous: strong feelings of love
Anachronism: a thing belonging or appropriate to a period other than that in which it exists
Anagram: a word or phrase formed by rearranging the letters of a different word or phrase, using all the letters exactly once
Anathema: something that is hated
Antagonist: to actively oppose something
Antipathy: strong dislike
Apathetic: showing or feeling no interest, enthusiasm, or concern
Aphorism- a pithy observation that contains a general truth
Apprehensive: anxious, fearful
Arbiter: a person who settles a dispute
Astute: ability to read situations & people and turn it to one's advantage
Atrophy: muscle becomes fat
Audacious- to take bold risks
Avarice: extreme greed for material gain
Badinage: humorous or playful
Befuddled: make someone unable to think clearly
Bellicose: demonstrating aggression and willingness to fight
Bestial: savagely cruel and depraved
Blasphemous: disrespectful sacred things; sacrilegious
Blemish: a small flaw that ruins the appearance of something
Blithe: cheerful and carefree
Bombastic: high-sounding but little meaning; inflated
Bronchi: any of the major air passages of the lungs
Browbeat: intimidate someone with stern or abusive words
Bungle: to carry out a task incompetently
Burly: a person large and strong built

Candiru- aka toothpick fish, or vampire fish, is a species of parasitic freshwater catfish native to the Amazon Basin
Captivate: attract & hold the attention of
Carouse: drink alcohol and party hard
Casuistry: use of clever but unsound reasoning
Cervix: narrow passage into uterus
Charisma: having great personal charm
Charlatan: a person falsely claiming to have a special knowledge or skill; a fraud
Chutzpah: shameless audacity; impudence
Cirrhosis: the liver does not function properly due to long-term damage, usually from alcohol
Complacent: overly content with one's achievements or actions
Condemn: express complete disapproval of, typically in public
Conjecture: an opinion or conclusion formed on the basis of incomplete information
Connoisseur: expert judge in matters of taste
Contemptuous: feeling that something is beneath consideration
Conundrum: a confusing and difficult problem or question
Coup D'etat: forcible removal of the existing government
Covert: not openly acknowledged or displayed
Credulous: too willing to believe things
Coy: Shyness or Modesty
Creed: to belief in or acceptance of something as true
Dapper: well-groomed, neat
Deft: skillful and quick in one's movement
Deleterious: harmful, often in a subtle or unexpected way
Deliberate: long consideration
Demigod: offspring of a god and a mortal
Détente- the easing of hostility or strained relations
Dexterity: skill using hands while doing tasks
Disdain: something or someone not worthy of respect
Dishearten- to depress or ruin one's hopes
Disheveled: untidy hair, clothes, or appearance
Disseminate: to spread information widely
Distraught: deeply upset & agitated
Dopamine: compound present in the body as a neurotransmitter; rewards user with a high
Ebullient: cheerful and full of energy
Ecclesiastical: relating to the Christian Church or its clergy
Echelon: a level in an organization

Effervescent: vivacious & enthusiastic
Effrontery- bold or impertinent behavior
Emphysema- a condition in which the air sacs of the lungs are damaged
Enchanted: placed under a spell; charmed
Envious: a feeling of resent aroused by someone else's possessions, qualities, or luck
Ephemeral: lasting only a very short time
Epitome: a person or thing that is the perfect example of a quality
Equanimity: mental calmness in a bad situation
Eradicate: destroy completely
Esoteric- likely to be understood by only a small number of people
Euphemism: a milder substitute for a word that is too harsh
Euphoric: intense feeling of excitement
Evasive: deceitful, trickery
Eviscerate: disembowel (person or animal); deprive something of its essence
Exalt: hold something in high regard
Exasperate: irritated & frustrated
Exhort: to strongly encourage or urge someone to do something
Expedite: make something happen sooner
Extol: praise enthusiastically
Extrapolate: reasoning the end point based on a trend
Exuberant: joyous
Fallopian Tube: pair of tubes along which eggs travel from the ovaries to the uterus.
Finesse: intricate & refined delicacy
Flabbergasted: surprised someone greatly
Flagellum: thin tail that enables swimming
Flamboyant: a person tending to attract attention because of their exuberance, confidence, and stylishness
Foray: an attack into enemy territory
Formidable: inspiring fear or respect through being large, powerful, intense, or capable
Fortuitous: lucky chance
Fraught: causing or affected by anxiety or stress
Frenetic: fast and energetic in a wild and uncontrolled way
Frenzy: uncontrolled state or situation
Gaffe: an unintentional act or remark causing embarrassment
Garrulous: talkative
Gene Edit- type of genetic engineering in which DNA is modified

Glutton: an excessively greedy eater
Gouge: overcharge; swindle; also, make a groove, hole or indentation
Grave: serious or dangerous
Haughty: arrogantly superior
Hedonist- a person who acts purely in the pursuit of pleasure
Highbrow: scholarly or rarefied in taste
Hyperbole: exaggerated statements
Ignominy: public shame or disgrace
Illusion: something wrongly perceived or interpreted by the senses
Impeccable: faultless
Imperious: assuming power or authority without justification
Implore: beg someone
Impunity: exempt from punishment; freedom from consequences
Inane: silly; stupid; empty; insubstantial
Inconceivable: can't be imagined
Incorrigible: a person or their tendencies not able to be corrected, improved, or reformed
Incredulous: a person unwilling or unable to believe something
Indignant: angered at unfair treatment
Indiscriminate: done at random
Infusion: drink made by soaking something in a liquid; introduce something new
Inoculate: vaccinate to become immune
Insipid: lacking flavor or vigor
Insular: ignorant of or uninterested in cultures, ideas, or peoples outside one's own experience
Involuntary: done without conscious control
that they cannot be made compatible
Irremediable: impossible to cure or put right
Irreverent: lack of respect for people or things normally taken seriously
Jest: a thing said or done for amusement
Jovial: cheerful and friendly
Jubilant: feeling or expressing great happiness and triumph
Kinetic Energy: Energy of Motion
Lambaste: criticize sharply
Lament: a passionate expression of grief
Lampoon: publicly criticize someone or something by using ridicule, irony, or sarcasm
Lascivious: showing an overt and often offensive sexual desire

Loathe: intense hatred
Loquacious: talkative
Lugubrious: looking or sounding sad
Luminary: a star who influences others
Machination: a plot or scheme
Malediction: a magical word or phrase uttered with the intention of bringing about evil or destruction; a curse
Masochism: to derive pleasure from one's own pain or humiliation
Maven: an expert
Mediator: a person who resolves a conflict
Megalomania: false impression of one's own greatness
Melodramatic: exaggerated or overemotional with small things
Metaphor: a thing regarded as representative or symbolic of something else, especially something abstract
Mien: a person's look or manner
Misanthrope: hater of mankind
Morph: to change from one form to another
Mortify: great embarrassment & shame
Multifaceted: having many talents
Musculo-Skeletal: Muscles & Skeleton (bones)
Narcissistic: having an excessive interest in oneself
Nebulous: hazy, cloudy
Nemesis: the inescapable agent of someone's or something's downfall
Neophyte: Beginner
Obscure: not discovered or known about
Officious: domineering over trivial matters
Ogle: stare at in a sensual manner
Oligarchy: a small group having control or power
Onomatopoeia: the formation of a word from a sound associated with what is named
Orthodoxy: generally accepted theory, doctrine, or practice
Ostracize: to exclude someone from a group
Panache: flamboyant confidence of style
Paroxysm: a sudden violent outburst
Pernicious: having a harmful effect, usually gradual or subtle.
Petulant: childishly sulky or bad mannered
Pilfer: to steal, especially in small quantities
Piquant: having a pleasantly sharp taste
Pituitary Gland: small pea-sized gland that secretes human growth hormone during puberty

Potential Energy: Stored Energy
Prepossessing: attractive in appearance
Prerequisite- a thing that is required as a prior condition for something else to happen
Presage: a sign or warning that something
Procure: to get by special effort
Prodigy: a young person exceptionally talented
Proletariat: working-class people
Promulgate: to promote or make known
Protean- tending to change frequently
Prototype: a first, typical or preliminary model of something, from which other forms are developed or copied
Puberty- the period during which adolescents reach sexual maturity
Pungent: having a strong taste or smell
Punitive: intended as punishment
Putative: supposed
Querulous: complaining and whining
Quibble: a slight objection or criticism about a trivial matter
Quixotic: foolishly romantic, unrealistic and impractical
Ramification: a consequence of an action or event, usually unwelcome
Rapacity: Excessively Greedy
Rectify: put something right; correct
Remorseful: feel guily or ashamed
Reputable: having a good reputation
Rudimentary: most basic form
Sagacious: having or showing keen judgment
Salacious: inappropriate interest in sex
Scatological: relating to excrement
Sedentary: tending to spend too much time without moving
Seditious: rebel against authority
Segregate: set apart from the rest or from the other; isolate
Serendipity: the occurrence and development by chance in a happy or beneficial way
Shrewd: showing sharp intellect and judgment
Skulk: out of sight, typically with a sinister or cowardly motive.
Smug: having or showing excessive pride in oneself or one's achievement
Snub: give someone the cold shoulder
Sophomoric: pretentious or juvenile
Spectacle: impressive visual impact

Stolid: a person who is calm, dependable, and showing little emotion or animation
Strenuous: requiring great exertion
Subterfuge: a trick to escape something unpleasant; ruse; artifice
Supercilious: acting superior to others
Surreptitious: secretive
Swoon: faint from extreme emotion
Sycophant: to suck up to gain favor
Terse: brief in speech
Trepidation: fear of something
Turgid: swollen and distended or congested
Unassuming: not claiming attention
Unencumber: not having any burden or impediment
Unflappable- showing determination when in a crisis
Unheralded: not recognized
Unkempt: unclean appearance
Unsuspecting: not aware of danger
Upend: to overthrow
Urethra: the duct by which urine is conveyed out of the body from the bladder, and which in male vertebrates also conveys semen
Utopia: ideal place and life
Vacuous: having or showing a lack of thought or intelligence
Vain: having or showing an excessively high opinion of one's appearance, abilities, or worth
Valiant: showing courage
Versatile: able to adapt to many different functions or activities
Vindicate: wanting revenge
Virulent: a disease or poison extremely severe or harmful
Viscosity: thickness of fluid

Related Words

Abdicate: renounce, forgo, relinquish, cede, abnegate, abjure, leave
Acerbic: caustic, harsh, sharp, acidic, tart, scatching, acrid, biting
Adroit: adept, deft, clever, artful, proficient, whiz, savvy, cunning
Agalmatophilia: sexual fetish, paraphilia, sadomasochism
Alacrity: alert, lively, prompt, eager, zeal, fervor, brisk, enthusiasm
Alliteration: repitition, recurrence, reiterate, rhyme, iterate
Aloof: remote, detached, standoffish, callous, distant, nonchalant
Alveoli: bronchi, lungs, pleura, respiratory, tracheal, thoracic,
Amorous: affectionate, erotic, romantic, sprung, doting, enamored
Anachronism: misplacement, chronological error, misdate, prolepsis
Anagram: puzzle, cipher, game, scrabble, double meaning
Anathema: bane, pariah, abomination, bugbear, detestation, enemy
Antagonist: adversary, nemesis, foe, rival, opposer, opponent
Antipathy: hostility, ill will, animosity, animus, aversion, antagonism
Apathetic: uncaring, callous, indifferent, passive, don't give a damn
Aphorism: adage, axiom, dictum, maxim, proverb, truism, saw, rule
Apprehensive: anxious, jittery, nervous, concerned, afraid
Arbiter: mediator, moderator, go-between, adjudicator, referee, fixer
Astute: perceptive, adroit, keen, shrewd, discerning, crafty, insightful
Atrophy: degenerate, decline, deteriorate, diminution, wearing, waste
Audacious: reckless, bold, adventurous, courageous, daredevil, brave
Avarice: greed, covetousness, cupidity, rapacity, penny-pinching
Badinage: banter, repartee, wordplay, witticisms, quip, bon mots
Befuddled: baffled, bewildered, dumbfounded, stupefied, obfuscate
Belie: contradict, negate, repudiate, distort, mislead, conceal, pervert
Bellicose: belligerent, hostile, pugnacious, pugilist, quarrelsome
Bestial: savage, barbarous, beastly, boorish, brutish, cruel, depraved
Blasphemous: irreverent, profane, sacrilegious, impious, ungodly
Blemish: flaw, blot, error, sully, stigma, deformity, imperfection
Blithe: carefree, jovial, lighthearted, buoyant, mirthful, jolly, chirpy
Bombastic: pompous, grandiloquent, grandiose, highfalutin,
Burly: husky, beefy, brawny, muscular, stocky, stout, beefcake
Cantankerous: crabby, cranky, grouchy, crotchety, irascible, prickly
Captivate: enchant, beguile, bewitch, charm, dazzle, allure, enrapture
Carouse: booze, imbibe, inebriate, revel, frolic, paint the town red
Casuistry: evasion, deception, glib, sophistry, equivocate, specious
Cattywampus: awry, askew, askance, cockeyed, crroked, off-center
Charisma: charm, allure, glamour, dazzle, magnetism, enchanting
Charlatan: swindler, con artist, mountebank, fraud, phony, quack

Chutzpah: arrogance, audacity, gall, boldness, fearlessness, spine
Complacent: content, pleased, satisfied, gratified, easy-going
Condemn: blame, castigate, censure, criticize, knock, deprecate
Conjecture: speculate, presume, hypothesize, guess, surmise
Connoisseur: authority, aficionado, dilettante, buff, expert, maven
Contemptuous: condescending, scornful, insulting, uppity, snooty
Covert: clandestine, surreptitious, concealed, cloaked, veiled, QT
Credulous: gullible, naïve, dupable, trustful, believing, unwary
Coy: shy, modest, bashful, timid, demure, diffident, blushing
Creed: belief, doctrine, dogma, faith, tenet, ideology, orthodoxy
Deft: adept, agile, clever, adroit, dexterous, skilled, able, nimble, apt
Deleterious: harmful, damaging, destructive, pernicious, detrimental
Deliberate: ponder, reflect, mull over, consult, ruminate, cogitate
Détente: easement, cease-fire, peace, de-escalation, truce, armistice
Disdain: derision, contempt, insolence, disparagement, antipathy
Dishearten: demoralize, deter, disparage, dampen, humiliate, depress
Disheveled: bedraggled, frowzy, rumpled, disarrayed, slovenly
Disseminate: circulate, propagate, diffuse, dissipate, scatter
Distraught: agitated, rattled, flustered, perturbed, tormented
Ebullient: zestful, effervescent, chipper, exuberant, vivacious
Ecclesiastical: churchly, clerical, religious, spiritual, holy, pastoral
Echelon: class, level, degree, file, grade, place, position, rank, tier
Effrontery: temerity, insolence, brazen, audacious, arrogant, gall
Ephemeral: fleeting, transitory, momentary, episodic, evanescent
Equanimity: aplomb, serenity, tranquility, sangfroid, composure
Eradicate: annihilate, expunge, extirpate, exterminate, eviscerate,
Esoteric: arcane, cryptic, mystical, obscure, recondite, inscrutable
Euphemism: flatter, inflation, floridness, pretense, grandiloquence
Exalt: laud, dignify, extol, revere, glorify, lionize, idolize, commend
Exhort: urge, admonish, beseech, implore, plead, advise, caution
Expedite: accelerate, assist, facilitate, hasten, precipitate, urge
Extrapolate: infer, hypothesize, anticipate, conclude, envision
Finesse: subtlety, savvy, acumen, skill, craftiness, artfulness
Flabbergast: astonish, astound, daze, disconcert, dumbfound, stagger
Flamboyant: extravagant, dazzling, fabulous, swanky, panache
Foray: incursion, invasion, attack, raid, sortie, strike, surprise attack
Formidable: terrifying, dreadful, imposing, menacing, impregnable
Fortuitous: lucky, serendipitous, fortunate, random, chance, luck out
Fraught: full of, charged, filled, replete, laden, bristling, abounding
Frenetic: maniacal, frantic, frenzied, weirded out, insane, distraught
Gaffe: blunder, blooper, indiscretion, goof, faux pas, indecorum

Garrulous: loquacious, verbose, prating, effusive, voluble, glib
Glutton: epicure, gorger, gourmand, hog, hedonist, heavy eater, pig
Gouge: groove, excavate, cut; also, swindle, hoodwink, extort, hoax
Grave: somber, solemn, serious, gloomy, sober, grim, staid, earnest
Haughty: arrogant, supercilious, hoity-toity, pretentious, imperious
Ignominy: disgrace, dishonor, direpute, humiliation, shame,
Illusion: chimera, deception, misconception, fantasy, apparition
Impeccable: immaculate, exquisite, infallible, unimpeachable
Impunity: freedom, immunity, exception, exemption, liberty
Inane: absurd, sophomoric, vacuous, harebrained, jejune, vapid
Inconceivable: extraordinary, implausible, improbable, incredible
Incorrigible: hopeless, irreparable, intractable, inveterate
Incredulous: skeptical, quizzical, dubious, wary, suspect
Indignant: irate, livid, peeved, piqued, miffed, resentful, scornful
Indiscriminate: random, aimless, haphazard, unselective, designless
Infusion: immersion, mixture, strain; also imbue, ingrain, inoculate
Inoculate: immunize, vaccinate, protect, resistant, safe, exempt
Insular: parochial, provincial, narrow-minded, bigoted, cut off
Involuntary: automatic, compulsory, conditioned, uncontrolled
Irremediable: hopeless, irredeemable, incurable, irreversible, fatal
Jest: joke, banter, gag, wisecrack, jive, quip, pleasantry, prank, rib
Lambaste: assail, berate, castigate, excoriate, scold, upbraid
Lament: mourn, bemoan, regret, grive, bewail, rue, weep, wail
Lampoon: satirize, parody, caricature, mock, roast, fry, burlesque
Lascivious: lewd, salacious, prurient, pornographic, vulgar, crass
Loathe: abhor, despise, detest, hate, abominate, spurn, condemn
Malediction: curse, hex, jinx, imprecation, voodoo, kiss of death,
Megalomania: egoism, arrogance, haughty, vain, narcissistic
Melodramatic: theatrical, artificial, sensational, histrionic
Mien: presence, manner, countenance, demeanor, appearance, aura
Misanthrope: cynic, doubter, hater, egoist, recluse, grinch-like
Morph: alter, modify, transform, transmute, distort, recast, malleable
Multifaceted: versatile, many-sided, protean, all-around, adaptable
Nebulous: ambiguous, amorphous, murky, hazy, imprecise, vague
Neophyte: beginner, novice, amateur, greenhorn, rookie, fledgling
Officious: impertinent, inquisitive, interfering, obstructive
Ogle: stare, gawk, gaze, glare, leer, gape at, rubberneck
Pilfer: filch, steal, appropriate, rob, snatch, purloin, swipe, embezzle
Piquant: peppery, pungent, savory, spicy, tangy, zesty
Prepossessing: attractive, handsome, dapper, debonair, dashing
Prerequisite: necessary, conditional, essential, imperative, obligatory

Procure: acquire, obtain, purchase, annex, solicit, get a hold of
Promulgate: declare, make known, disseminate, broadcast, proclaim
Prototype: antecedent, archtype, precedent, standard, model
Pun: play on words, double entendre, joke, quip, double meaning
Punitive: disciplinary, penal, punishing, punitory, vindictive
Querulous: complaining, bemoaning, carping, irritable, petulant
Quibble: object, bicker, carp, squabble, waffle, wrangle, pettifog
Ramification: consequence, aftermath, sequel, result, outsome, effect
Rectify: amend, fix, remedy, redress, reform, mend, repair, correct
Remorseful: penitent, sorrowful, regretful, contrite, apologetic
Rudimentary: elemental, elementary, introductory, fundamental
Seditious: rebellious, subversive, treasonous, iconoclast, dissident
Skulk: lurk, prowl, creep, slink, snoop, lie in wait
Snub: boycott, disregard, pass up, shun, scorn, slight, ice out
Spectacle: demonstration, display, drama, event, sight, extravaganza
Stolid: stoic, impassive, inactive, passive, unexcitable, indifferent
Strenuous: arduous, demanding, laborious, taxing, toilsome
Subterfuge: ploy, bluff, hoax, sham, artifice, ruse, stratagem
Sycophant: groupie, lackey, flatterer, fawner, bootlicker, conformist
Trepidation: apprehension, consternation, dismay, agitation, fright
Turgid: swollen, bloated, distended, tumid, puffy, tumescent
Unencumber: free, unburdened, clear, unblock, liberated
Unheralded: unsung, anonymous, slept on, overlooked, underrated
Unsuspecting: unwitting, innocent, gullible, trustful, naïve
Upend: invalidate, nullify, repeal, invert, upset, reverse, coutermand
Utopia: bliss, paradise, eden, shangri-la, arcadia, wonderland, heaven
Valiant: brave, courageous, gutsy, intrepid, plucky, valorous
Virulent: poisonous, pernicious, venemous, vitriolic, acrimonious

Attributions

Material Used to create work

Effrontery: Creative Commons Attribution 3.0 License; The Absolute Loser; MasaBowser
https://www.deviantart.com/masabowser/art/The-Absolute-Loser-176072969
Effervescent: Cristiano Ronaldo; 6456464545645; Creative Commons Attribution 3.0 License; CR7- Real Madrid by namo; 445578gfx
https://www.deviantart.com/445578gfx/art/6456464545645-780287022
Snub: DeviantArt
Super Girl: Creative Commons Attribution 3.0 License; emy lee69
Superman Premium Format: Creative Commons Attribution 3.0 License; DavidBaldo
DCSHG-2019-WonderWoman; Creative Commons Attribution-Share Alike 3.0 License; FigyaLova
Spiderman: Spidey; Creative Commons Attribution 3.0 License; hoyle600
Supergirl: https://www.deviantart.com/emy-lee69/art/super-girl-69793387
Superman: https://www.deviantart.com/davidbaldo/art/Superman-Premium-Format-585968820
WonderWoman: https://www.deviantart.com/figyalova/art/DCSHG-2019-Wonder-Woman-788200094
Spiderman: https://www.deviantart.com/hoyle600/art/Spidey-667017871
https://www.davidmarquez.com/
Rapacity: First Squirrel Assassin; shotokanteddy; Creative Commons Attribution 3.0 License
https://www.deviantart.com/shotokanteddy/art/First-Squirrel-Assassin-152927168
Flabbergasted: Attribution 2.0 Generic (CC by 2.0); DonkeyHotey
https://www.flickr.com/photos/donkeyhotey/
https://www.flickr.com/photos/donkeyhotey/21789121939/
Apprehensive: Creative Commons Attribution 3.0 License; OleGrayMane
https://www.deviantart.com/olegraymane/art/Ren-and-Stimpy-Happy-Helmet-316589765
Détente: Common Attribution-Share Alike 3.0 License; Ryu Street Fighter; Kid356 Creative Commons Attribution 3.0 License; Blaire Dame; evatge1984
Ryu: https://www.deviantart.com/kid356/art/Ryu-Street-Fighter-145365647
Blair Dame https://www.deviantart.com/evatge1984/art/Blair-Dame-176482128
Eradicate: Battle Angel Alita; Creative Commons Attribution-Share Alike 3.0 License; MsAnnThrope
https://www.deviantart.com/msannthrope/art/Battle-Angel-Alita-462596058
Adroit: Mayweather vs McGregor Poster; Creative Commons Attribution 3.0 License; WWESlashrocker54
https://www.deviantart.com/wweslashrocker54/art/Mayweather-vs-McGregor-Poster-632611829
Multifaceted: HDYB-FDOS Clawdeen Wolf (Alt Version); Creative Commons Attribution-Share Alike 3.0 License; FigyaLova
https://www.deviantart.com/figyalova/art/HDYB-FDOS-Clawdeen-Wolf-Alt-Version-672621915
Epitome:
Goku: CC Attribution; from chinese mobile game; Nemix
Roadrunner: To Beep or Not to Beep; Fair Use

Sonic: Wikifur; CC-BY-SA
Flash: Young justice legacy 3d models; Creative Commons Attribution 3.0 License; FuncoHD
Goku https://sketchfab.com/3d-models/goku-6a79ab6b70b747b68e787da1458ab582
Roadrunner:https://ms.wikipedia.org/wiki/Wile_E._Coyote_dan_Road_Runner#/media/Fail:Roadrunner.gif
Sonic: https://en.wikifur.com/wiki/Sonic_the_Hedgehog_(character)
Flash: https://www.deviantart.com/funcohd/art/Young-justice-legacy-3d-models-419136411
Jovial: Elf: CC-BY-SA
https://elf.fandom.com/wiki/Buddy
Santa: https://sobernation.com/gearing-holidays/
Santa's Workshop: https://mailchi.mp/7f96961edcbe/calebs-landing-page-for-all-your-needs
Prototype: Jeremy Lin in Preseason Vs. Indiana Pacers; Creative Commons Attribution-No Derivative Works 3.0 License; THEMADJUMP
https://www.deviantart.com/themadjump/art/JEREMY-LIN-IN-PRESEASON-Vs-INDIANA-PACERS-406597169
Officious: Creative Commons Attribution-Shares Alike License 3.0 CC-BY-SA; Simpsons Wiki
https://simpsons.fandom.com/wiki/Coach_Krupt
Antipathy: Blogspot
https://www.mens-corner.net/2015/11/scientists-prove-women-nagging-shorten.html
Disdain: https://solvibrations.org/help-relieve-snoring/
Indignant: CC BY 2.0
https://www.flickr.com/photos/8136496@N05/2099062718
Distraught: CC BY 2.0; Philip Robertson
https://www.flickr.com/photos/philiprobertson/9791303373
Coy: My Hero Academia: Izuku Midoriya (Deku); Creative Commons Attribution-Share Alike 3.0 License; Zargorth
https://www.deviantart.com/zargorth/art/My-Hero-Academia-Izuku-Midoriya-Deku-practice-702470712
Enchanted: CC BY-SA; The1stMoyatia
https://www.deviantart.com/the1stmoyatia/art/JessicaRabbit-451444013
Flamboyant: Creative Commons Attribution-Share Alike License 3.0; CC-BY-SA; Wiki Simpsons
https://simpsonswiki.com/wiki/Queen_Chante
Frenzy: CC-BY-SA; SuperMelon
https://www.generasia.com/wiki/File:BTS_-_Map_of_the_Soul_7_~The_Journey~_promo.jpg
Unassuming: NFL Football and Sports Photos; Creative Commons Attribution Share Alike 3.0 License; NFLNewsDesk
https://www.deviantart.com/nflnewsdesk/art/NFL-Football-and-Sports-Photos-341673908
Dexterity: Creative Commons Attribution- No Derivative Works 3.0 License; Fraviro
https://www.deviantart.com/fraviro/art/Greek-Freak-Zone-739142019
Versatile: - Creative Commons 3.0; EduArts16
https://www.deviantart.com/eduarts16/art/Taylor-Swift-554151544
Panache:
Bikini Stevonnie: Creative Commons Attribution- Share Alike 3.0 License; Rayryan90

https://www.deviantart.com/rayryan90/art/Bikini-Stevonnie-621862377
Protean: Pennwise; Creative Commons Attribution-Share Alike 3.0 License; juhoham
https://www.deviantart.com/juhoham/art/Pennywise-405055417
Esoteric: Illuminati control over mind wallpaper; Creative Commons Attribution-Share Alike 3.0 License; DemiPsycho
https://www.deviantart.com/demipsycho/art/Illuminati-control-over-mind-Wallpaper-405103881
Grave: Pubertina Anime; Creative Commons Attribution 3.0 License; Rockstarlucero
https://www.deviantart.com/rockstarlucero/art/Pubertina-Anime-312895001
Charisma: This file was imported from TV Tropes in July 2012, when all of their site content was licensed under the Creative Commons Attribution-Share Alike 3.0 Unported license (CC-BY-SA 3.0).
Exasperate: https://crazyneel.wordpress.com/lifes-like-that/never-start-a-project-unless-all-resources-are-available/
Vain: https://polokiller.wordpress.com/
Querulous: The Solar System; Creative Commons Attribution 3.0 License; ValiantPenguin
https://www.deviantart.com/valiantpenguin/art/The-Solar-System-484294484
Remorseful: Superman vs Batman; Creative Commons Attribution-Share Alike 3.0 License; BoredomKillsinc
https://www.deviantart.com/boredomkillsinc/art/Superman-vs-Batman-294599251
Jubilant: CC BY-SA 4.0; Nicholas Moreau; File:Anime North 2017 animegao c IMG 5076.jpg
https://en.wikipedia.org/wiki/Animegao_kigurumi#/media/File:Anime_North_2017_animegao_c_IMG_5076.jpg
Luminary: Lionel Messi; Creative Commons Attribution 3.0 License; apelaths
https://www.deviantart.com/apelaths/art/LIONEL-MESSI-550643870
Garrulous: Content is available under Attribution-Share Alike 3.0 Unported
https://theinfosphere.org/File:Put_your_head_on_my_shoulder.jpg
Ignominy: https://wikiclipart.com/cornhole-clipart_26224/
Avarice: People Fighting Over Money is free clipart uploaded by user. Its resolution is 722PX x 480PX pixels. Download it free for your creative projects.
https://www.netclipart.com/isee/iiRmJTi_people-fighting-over-money/
Presage: Monstara
https://www.deviantart.com/monstara/art/STD-Cartoon-24016915
Haughty (American Progress-John Gast): Creative Commons Attribution-ShareAlike License
https://en.wikipedia.org/wiki/American_Progress#/media/File:American_Progress_(John_Gast_painting).jpg
Prodigy: 1100 Kyrie Irving by namo,7; Creative Commons Attribution 3.0 License; 445578gfx
https://www.deviantart.com/445578gfx/art/1100-Kyrie-Irving-by-namo-7-490229313
Jest: Creative Commons CC0
https://commons.wikimedia.org/wiki/Category:Hypertrichosis?uselang=de
Atrophy: CC-BY-SA-4.0; Vectortoons
https://commons.wikimedia.org/wiki/File:Old_Cartoon_Man_Using_A_Big_Computer.svg
Finesse: Roger Federer wallpaper by namo, 7-000800; Creative Commons Attribution 3.0 License; 445578gfx

https://www.deviantart.com/445578gfx/art/Roger-Federer-wallpaper-by-namo-7-000800-360155219
Upend: National Print Museum- No Copyright Restrictions
https://www.irishtimes.com/culture/heritage/how-irish-women-won-the-right-to-vote-in-1918-1.3697389
https://www.flickr.com/photos/lselibrary/26165613708/
Anathema: CC BY-SA 2.0; Christopher Johnson; IMG_4306_2
https://fr.wikipedia.org/wiki/Mike_Krzyzewski#/media/Fichier:Mike_Krzyzewski_incrependo_a_alguien_en_un_partido_del_Mundial_de_baloncesto_2010.jpg
Duke Logo: Creative Commons CC0 License
https://commons.wikimedia.org/wiki/File:Duke_Blue_Devils_logo.svg
Ostracized: Karate Kid; Creative Commons Attribution-Share Alike 3.0 License; BoogieNightBoy; Pat Morita e Daniel San
https://www.deviantart.com/boggienightboy/art/KARATE-KID-367081801
Supercilious: Ninja Turtles; Fair Use
https://en.wikipedia.org/wiki/Teenage_Mutant_Ninja_Turtles

Attributions for material used as reference to create derivative works
Condemn - individual personality images via CC licensing. All works are derivative works.
Polk - WikiPedia - CC0 1.0 Universal (CC0 1.0) Public Domain Dedication
Andre_Agassi_1999 - CC BY SA 2.0
 Kingkongphoto & www.celebrity-photos.com from Laurel Maryland, USA
Nicolas_Cage_2011_CC BY SA 2.0
 Gerald Geronimo at https://www.flickr.com/people/25445109@N07
David_Bowie_-_TopPop_1974_08 - CC BY SA 3.0
 David_Bowie_-_TopPop_1974_08.png
John_T_color_01 (John Travolta) CC-BY-SA 3.0
 Author Towpilot
Paul_and_Linda_McCartney_Wings_Over_America_1976_
 By Capitol Records - eBayfrontback, Public Domain
Derivative individual images declared free to use by Creative Commons, no restrictions
Deleterious
Shutterstock - image 124820158
Ecclesiastical
MOMA NY Adoration of the Magi From Seven Scenes From the Life of Christ - via netgear.
Eviscerate
Shutterstock - image 1175517274
Quid Pro Quo
shutterstock - image 116101606
Retribution
Alamy - image BC6XCN
canstock - image 61393750
Vacuous
shutterstock - image 176126231
All complete image derivative works: Copyright Northeast By Southwest, Inc.

About AbVocab Publishing, Inc.

Abvocab was co-founded by Matt Quenville and Northeast by Southwest, Inc. in February 2020 to produce, promote and sell Vocabulary based products, including books, interactive websites and general merchandise. In particular, Abocab uses imaginative visuals and usage sentences to engage learners young, old and everyone in between. General Email: info@abvocabpublishing.com

About the Co-Founders

President, Matt Quenville is an educator and entrepreneur. He teaches History at a middle school in Virginia. He currently lives with his wife and 2 children in Hampton Roads, Virginia, where he owns and operates Little Piggy's Wurst Nightmare food trucks and catering. His inspiration for his study book to be soon published was sparked by the lack of engaging vocabulary study guides for the Graduate Record Exam.

Email: M.T.Quenville@abvocabpublishing.com

Vice President, Sketchi Bill, aka Bill Unkel, aka Dr. William C. Unkel has been an educator, scientist/engineer, businessman and the creator of SketchiToons®. Over the years Bill has worked in areas from Plasma Physics to America's Cup technology. His companies have produced science software, unique daylight viewable computer screens and 'Smart Meters.' He currently lives and plays around the city of Santa Fe, New Mexico. Other books by Sketchi Bill are available on Amazon and at www.sketchitoons.com

Email: W.C.Unkel@abvocabpublishing.com

New AbVocab Offering
Sketchi CrossWords™
By Sketchi Bill

Whether you do crosswords or not, the clues and answers of the NY Times crosswords offer a rich selection of interesting words often with a pun or two. The book will include SketchiToons® with words often from the difficult Friday and Saturday puzzles.

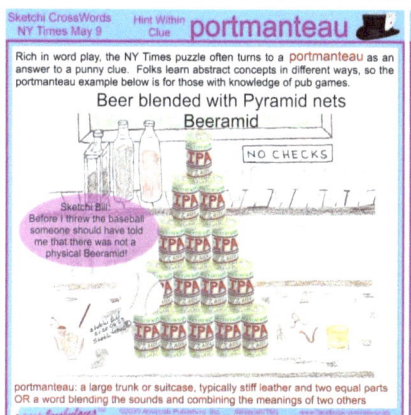
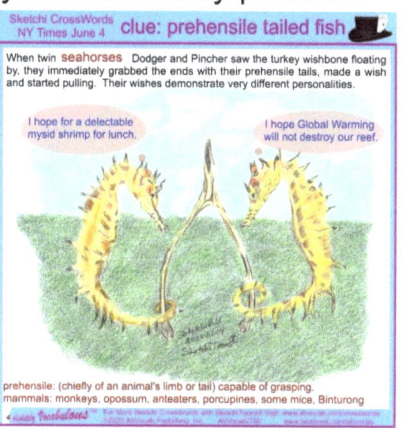

Check out the book entries as they appear online and on Facebook. Some will be 'timely' and helpful if you are doing the puzzles.
Fun way to reconnect and to become Absolutely Vocabulous.

Visit: www.abvocab.com/crosswords
and @Absolutely Vocabulous on FB

An *Absolutely Vocabulous*™ Production

Available Now On Amazon
Wait! Wait! I Know That Word!
By Sketchi Bill and Matt Quenville
with SketchiToons® by Sketchi Bill

A humorous and sometimes irreverent picture book where sketches and quips connect you with words to engage family, friends, co-workers, bosses and kids.

Don't be in a Quandary when expressing yourself.

Visit: www.abvocab.com/buy-stuff or On Amazon Look for Sketchi Bill or Matt Quenville

www.ingramcontent.com/pod-product-compliance
Lightning Source LLC
Chambersburg PA
CBHW040847170426
43201CB00005BB/48